ARTEM KUDELIA PHD

Breathwork Therapy Seminar

Holotropic Journey to Unconscious Mind Secrets

First edition

This book was professionally typeset on Reedsy.
Find out more at reedsy.com

Contents

Foreword

This book presents a transcript of a seminar on Holotropic breathwork, one of the well-known therapeutic methods developed by Stanislav and Christina Grof in the 1960s. Readers are invited to explore the method's intricacies, nuances, and distinctive features. The book includes feedback from therapy session participants, providing detailed accounts of their transpersonal experiences during the Holotropic breathwork process.

This book is recommended for psychologists, psychotherapists, medical professionals, philosophers, and a broader readership interested in the field of psychotherapy.

Holotropic breathwork, both as a psychotherapeutic approach and a means of self-exploration, was developed by Stanislav and Christina Grof in the 1960s and 1970s at the Esalen Institute in Big Sur, California. In contrast to the predominantly verbal methods commonly associated with classical psychoanalysis, Holotropic breathwork enables the direct expression of a client's emotions and feelings. The creators of this approach discovered and successfully employed a remarkable method for activating the therapeutic potential and healing power of what they termed "holotropic states of consciousness" in their clients.

For academic psychology, this discovery proved immensely valuable. Researchers worldwide became intrigued by this new understanding of both healthy and pathological aspects of the human psyche, as well as the deep-seated foundations of human consciousness. Access to autobiographical experiences, including the perinatal period, became available. Entirely new possibilities for practical exploration and scientific conceptualization of transpersonal domains within the unconscious psyche emerged.

Prolonged conscious breathing leads to a "healing event" over time—distinct changes in both the individual and their psyche that release energy associated with various traumatic memories. This energy finds external expression and can be constructively processed.

This book is dedicated to the art of inducing such "healing events" in psychotherapeutic work with clients. It is a concise and engaging narrative, reflecting the author's own psychotherapeutic experiences, structured around the "days of the seminar."

The narrative begins with a description of the "external," the "known" motivator that led the Great Master to create the psychotherapeutic approach known as Holotropic breathwork (the prohibition of LSD-25, in the words of Aleksei Leontiev). However, beneath this external motivator, one can readily discern an "internal," a "genuinely operative" motive: Stanislav Grof's desire to help people take more effective care of themselves, enhance the quantity and quality of their health, and make illness their teacher.

The book skillfully balances lucidly presented "theoretical" aspects with meticulously detailed "practical" components of working with the Holotropic method. The theory gently immerses the reader in the context of various facets of employing the Holotropic method, while the practical aspects are depicted in such a way that the reader becomes a participant in a "live process," a "witness to therapy."

This book will captivate both readers encountering the Holotropic approach in psychotherapy for the first time and those who wish to "experiment" with a method they are already familiar with theoretically. Experienced psychotherapists who have applied the Holotropic approach in their practice will also discover valuable insights, allowing them to validate their own experiences against those of the author in this book.

One more noteworthy aspect is the trust in the text that inevitably arises during reading. The author of this book has a personal connection to the "primary source"—the creator of Holotropic breathwork. He received information "firsthand," and thanks to his efforts, we can hear the original voice.

Preface

The book you are holding in your hands was conceived as a transcript of one of the Holotropic breathwork seminars we conducted in 2018. In the context of working with various groups using the Holotropic breathwork method, it is possible to attain a vivid, colorful, and profound experience, and naturally, there arises a desire to immortalize it in printed form. Despite the relatively modest size of this work, it pursues several goals that are significant to us. These include:

- Providing readers with a general introduction to the Holotropic breathwork method and its developmental history.
- Describing the specifics of its implementation and the key aspects of the therapist's behavior and the session environment, which can be important and relevant.
- Demonstrating and describing the experiences that individuals can gain during Holotropic breathwork through verbal feedback and artwork.
- Describing the techniques for working with a patient's body during Holotropic breathwork, if such a need arises.
- Offering a comprehensive description of what happens to a person's physiology when they initiate the hyperventilation process in their lungs through breathwork.

We hope that this work will provide the reader with both practical knowledge of the Holotropic breathwork method on an intellectual level and enjoyment from reading it.

Acknowledgments

I would like to express my gratitude to my psychology and psychotherapy teachers, who have opened the path and laid a solid foundation of knowledge. Furthermore, I extend my immense appreciation to patients, colleagues, friends, and all individuals who have directly or indirectly contributed to the writing of this book.

BONUS: Get Your Free Resources Now

I'm excited to share a **free eBook** and **exclusive access** to **psychological resources** with you. To get started, scan the QR code or visit psychemaster.com/breathwork-therapy-seminar

What You'll Get:

- **Free eBook**: Explore advanced psychotherapeutic techniques and approaches that complement the insights.
- **Interactive Learning**: Engage with exercises and quizzes to solidify your understanding of complex theories.
- **Latest Research**: Stay updated with the most recent findings in the field of psychotherapy and integrative therapy approaches.
- **Continuous Support**: Get consistent tips, strategies, and motivation to assist you in staying focused and excelling in your studies and practice.

Maximize your understanding of psychotherapy!

Day One: Lecture One

Holotropic breathwork is a transpersonal therapeutic method created by Stanislav Grof in the mid-1960s. At its core, this method involves inducing altered states of consciousness through the process of lung hyperventilation. This process imparts specific functions to our consciousness and mind. Let's start from the beginning. How did S. Grof come to develop this method? In what way did he aspire to use this method for healing and transforming others?

The history is quite ancient, dating back to the mid-1930s. It all began with a chemist named Albert Hofmann, who worked in a Swiss laboratory. He was conducting a chemical analysis of a parasitic plant known as ergot, which grew on wheat stems, with the aim of identifying the specific chemical alkaloids it might contain. Ergot had long been used in folk medicine and was one of the substances used to induce contractions during childbirth. For instance, it was administered to women struggling with labor, increasing the intensity of contractions.

Chemists have long sought substances that play a role in folk healing practices, attempting to isolate the specific chemical elements that truly influence transformative processes.

While working with ergot, A. Hofmann synthesized over 40 alkaloids, which he tested on laboratory rats. Initially, alkaloid number 25 did not attract much of Hofmann's attention. The rats, after receiving this substance, exhibited no extraordinary changes in physiology or behavior; they remained calm and composed. Hofmann left this synthesized substance in the archives and returned to it only seven years later. Conducting further research, Hofmann made an astonishing, somewhat uncharacteristic oversight for a chemist of his caliber: he accidentally touched his eye while wearing rubber laboratory gloves, and minute particles of the synthesized substance were transferred to his eye.

After some time, Hofmann experienced profoundly unique states of reality. Surprisingly, these experiences manifested not in the laboratory but on his way home, peacefully pedaling his bicycle. When he reached home, the extraordinary altered state of consciousness reached its zenith. Hofmann locked himself in his room, fearing he was going insane. This "journey" persisted for approximately four hours, during which Hofmann traversed the most incredible and extraordinary states. He experienced intense hallucinations and various paranoid fantasies. He began to believe that his neighbor, who lived across the street, was a witch casting spells on him. After a while, his state stabilized and returned to normal.

In hindsight, as Hofmann realized the causes of his unusual experience and reflected upon his astonishing scientific oversight, he decided to intentionally replicate his journey.

Returning to the laboratory, he resolved to ingest a minuscule (in his view) dose of the substance he had synthesized, unaware at the time that his "minuscule" dose was, in fact, a moderate dose for this particular substance, capable of inducing a profound hallucinogenic experience. Hofmann, at that point, did not yet fathom that he had stumbled upon one of the most potent hallucinogens known to science. Approximately 30 to 40 minutes later, he found himself once again immersed in the vortex of transpersonal experiences.

Inspired by the compound and its effects, Hofmann conducted a series of self-experiments, testing different dosages. He discovered that the minimum amount of the substance capable of inducing mild hallucinatory experiences was 50 micrograms (mcg).

Realizing the potential of his creation, he submitted a report of his experiments with his invention to familiar psychiatrists, who subsequently initiated investigations into testing this substance on mentally ill individuals. They believed that undergoing such "shock-like" experiences could help improve the dynamics of symptoms.

These studies continued for over 20 years, taking place in numerous clinics and laboratories across Europe and America. Over time, many physician-psychotherapists developed their own proprietary methods of treating patients using this substance. Some created entirely new, unique treatment approaches, while others simply integrated LSD-25 into existing psychotherapeutic practices. The avenues of treatment in psychiatry and psychotherapy with the aid of LSD-25 were numerous. In this seminar, we will briefly discuss two primary directions of LSD therapy: psycholytic therapy and psychedelic therapy.

Psycholytic therapy primarily involved administering minimal doses of LSD-25, typically around 50 micrograms. This allowed the patient to remain in a state where they did not enter deep transpersonal experiences but maintained heightened consciousness and mental openness. This facilitated freer association and a different understanding of the problem. Patients often underwent hundreds of psycholytic therapy sessions, sometimes exceeding this number. Physicians observing these patients over time did not detect any negative consequences of prolonged exposure to LSD-25 on the body and consciousness. Abstinence syndrome did not occur, and patients easily discontinued the use of the substance.

On the other hand, psychedelic therapy aimed for shorter treatment periods with "impactful" doses of the substance. Therapists worked with patients for up to twenty sessions, administering doses ranging from 250 mcg to as high as 15,000 mcg. This allowed patients to fully re-experience the liberating aspects of their subconscious, with therapists intervening only occasionally when deemed necessary.

During that time, in certain European countries, medical students even had the opportunity to take LSD-25 for educational purposes. There was an (albeit somewhat incorrect) belief that the states of consciousness induced by LSD-25 resembled the natural states of schizophrenics. Therefore, by personally experiencing these states, medical professionals could better understand the condition. In an educational context, psychiatrists could take LSD-25 up to three times.

Stanislav Grof, at that time, was one of the pioneering researchers of this substance. He not only tested it on himself but also actively developed techniques and practices for treating mentally ill individuals using LSD-25. Based on his research in this field, he authored numerous scientific works and earned a doctorate in medical sciences. S. Grof continued working with LSD therapy until the mid-1960s, when this substance became prohibited not only for recreational use but also for therapeutic purposes.

But why did a substance that had been actively utilized in

psychotherapy for over two decades suddenly fall into disuse and acquire the stigma of being one of the most harmful narcotics?

The excessive and widespread use of the substance among the general population led to numerous unfortunate incidents involving individuals under the influence of the substance. LSD-25 affects individuals in such a way that it excessively intensifies any incoming sensory stimuli. If a person takes the substance in a pleasant setting, listens to melodious ethnic music, and inhales the aroma of incense, the hallucinogenic journey results in warm, gentle reflections of suppressed "good" fragments of the subconscious. However, if the context of consumption resembles that of a drug den, the outcomes of the internal journey can be horrifying.

At this time, S. Grof, like all other therapists who employed LSD-25 in their practice, lost one of the primary tools of their therapeutic method. In search of an adequate replacement for this banned therapeutic approach, Stanislav Grof and his wife, Christina, turned their attention to yogic breathing practices. From these practices, they adopted a breathing technique that could induce states resembling those created during the consumption of LSD-25.

Thus emerged Holotropic Breathwork therapy, which can be roughly translated from Greek as "therapy of moving towards wholeness."

LSD began to spread beyond clinical settings in America and Europe when American intelligence agencies actively started testing the substance on individuals unrelated to clinics. They assembled specific experimental groups, inviting individuals, often students, willing to take LSD for $10 a night and provide comprehensive feedback on their experiences.

By the mid-1960s, LSD had gained popularity across America. More than 5 million Americans were using LSD on Saturday evenings. They would drop it on sugar cubes and consume it during lively parties. What makes LSD appealing, and what are its significant drawbacks?

LSD releases certain centers in our minds linked to the deeper layers of our unconscious. The substance acts as a trigger or hook, activating what lies deep within our consciousness and neurophysiology. If you have suppressed aggressive feelings, they will surface. If you have repressed feelings of fear or dread, they will emerge. If you have suppressed feelings of disgust, homicidal impulses, or various other states, they too will manifest during LSD intoxication.

The content of your unconscious begins to surface, and if this emergence is guided by an experienced psychotherapist, it can yield magnificent healing effects. However, when this is done outside of a medical context, it can lead to significant psychological trauma and push individuals toward deviant behavior that may culminate in tragedy.

Another advantage and disadvantage of LSD is that any interactions with the external world become exaggerated. For instance, if you hear vibrant, colorful music, that music becomes even more vivid and captivating. It generates images that accompany the music, an effect characterized by heightened sensory experiences. Furthermore, if you encounter someone very pleasant, see a fantastic, magnificent painting, or inhale Indian incense, you undergo a powerful hallucinatory effect that complements these sensations.

Any amplification of sensations occurs during LSD intoxication. However, if you find yourself in an alley surrounded by garbage cans, vomit, and homeless individuals or drug addicts, the sensory overload can create a sensory hell from which escaping may not be straightforward. People are extremely sensitive at this moment, susceptible to any form of suggestion or influence, which makes this state quite perilous.

Because individuals took this substance outside the confines of clinics, without the involvement of a psychotherapist, they would sooner or later experience what became known as a "bad trip." A bad trip involves journeying into the realms of one's fears, revulsions, anger, and horrifying demonic imagery. According to statistics, approximately one out of every four individuals taking LSD would have a bad trip. Some might jump out of windows, while others could throw themselves under cars or end their lives through various means.

Around 1967, the President of the United States classified LSD-25 as one of the most dangerous drugs, equating it with heroin, despite its complete dissimilarity in effects. At that time, over five million Americans were regular LSD users, and the hippie movement was in full swing.

The substance was not only removed from legal circulation, but clinical research related to it was also blocked. Therapeutic groups employing LSD in their practice were shuttered, and any research and scientific programs dedicated to LSD were halted.

Stanislav Grof, with his research into LSD therapy coming to an end, embarked on a quest for new ways to legally achieve altered states of consciousness. These states needed to offer therapeutic benefits while bearing at least some resemblance to the effects of LSD. After some time, his quest bore fruit.

Grof, along with his wife Christina, began exploring various techniques and practices rooted in shamanic and Indian traditions. Eventually, he managed to create an intriguing therapy method, incorporating a breathing technique from yoga that had been used by Indians in their spiritual practice for hundreds, possibly thousands, of years. He selected one specific technique and transformed it into the central practice of his new therapy.

Subsequently, he gradually tested his novel method, initially on himself and later on his patients, yielding increasingly constructive results. This method came to be known as "Holotropic Breathwork."

What does it entail? The structure of Holotropic Breathwork closely resembles psychedelic therapy with LSD, albeit without pharmacological stimulation. A group of people gathers, as we have here, and they employ mattresses on which they engage in the process of breathing. Ethnic music is played, guiding the effects and actions and states that individuals experience. A psychotherapist supervises the group and provides necessary support in case of any needs.

Throughout the breathing process, individuals may manifest various forms of emotional release. Any suppressed feelings hold significance, and it is crucial for them to find constructive outlets during the breathing session, which typically lasts 45 to 90 minutes. These expressions may include screams, cries, moans, striking the mattress, stomping feet, and more. Some patients may even experience expressions of sexual feelings.

Here we encounter another important concept in psychotherapy: the idea that a person suffers to the extent that they suppress specific emotions. Allowing these emotions to emerge intensely at a specific moment can limit them; they can be fully processed, and they become less overwhelming.

Feelings of anger, aggression, and other emotions are always within a certain limit. For instance, in my work with individuals, I often mention that if someone has experienced a single traumatic event, such as a severe beating or rape, or if they were subjected to sexual interactions during childhood, their transformational processes may involve just a few sessions. In these sessions, individuals may enter specific new, unusual states that have varying degrees of healing impact.

If we see, for example, patients who have been beaten for extremely long periods of time, a girl who is beaten by her stepfather throughout her childhood, every week, regularly, for prophylaxis. Then, during a Holotropic Breathing session, the patient, in the process of breathing, can to some extent reduce the emotional tension that has been the imprint of many emotional and physical traumas. One such patient screamed like this for about three seminars in a row—more than ten hours of screaming. My wall in the office space was dented from her hand strikes, which she made while doing holotropic breathing. She was hitting her arms and legs in all directions. Some of the punches went to me. The anger came out over ten hours—it was a period of abreaction. Only after the tenth hour of the holotropic session did she manage to enter a more calm and relaxed state in which she felt comfortable. Here we see a certain interesting tendency: the person must somehow integrate and unify certain parts of their personality that have been chipped away from them. For example, a part of the personality that has to do with the imprint of the aggressor, or a part of the personality associated with the abuser, is tied to a certain emotional abuse that occurred in childhood.

Another interesting case was with one of my students who was trying to give a seminar presentation. As soon as she started to speak, she would burst into tears and sobs. After a while, she would run out of the room. Then she would come back in, make another attempt to speak, and again it would go in circles. I started to tease her a little bit: "Come on, come on, you can do it; I know you can." After a while of this light teasing, she emotionally exploded again and stopped trying. She began to feel like I was performing aggressive sexual acts on her. I said, "Well, how long have you been having these emotions, Olivia?" She replied, "I've always been able to perform in school, but the total crap happens when I go out in front of a large audience. I get tremors, and I feel like someone might beat me up." I said, "Okay, Olivia, come to therapy with me." We worked in group therapy for a while, then in individual therapy. In her personal history, I discovered that she had been repeatedly beaten by her parents and relatives. She was repeatedly molested by certain members of her own family. She could, for example, recount the following: "Just recently, I came home and my grandfather was lying there, and he said, 'Let's watch TV.'" She lies down next to him and notices that her hand is on his penis. Then she gets scared and pulls her hand away. At the age of five, for not doing her homework, her father once just threw her on the bed and beat her severely. This has happened to her repeatedly. Her mother is in a psychiatric hospital with a diagnosis of schizophrenia. It's a very pathological family. The girl experiences extreme panic attacks.

I invited her to a holotropic breathing session, and she tried breathing. Starting the breathing process, she experienced very strange states. She had the most unusual states of reality occurring in her mind. Her face was continuously distorted by demonopathic masks. The most varied grimaces arose, which, in appearance, resembled some dark and gloomy mythical characters.

Such feelings can often be seen on the faces of people who have undergone elements of sexual abuse in childhood. They occur when a part of the personality that reproduces the pain and suffering that was inflicted on that person manifests.

She began to show a manifestation of the demonic part of her personality that contained destructive childhood experiences.

By and large, such effects and phenomena can occur very often in clinical practice. After some time, the girl completely freezes during breathing and has mild forms of epileptoid seizures. After a while, she completely loses her breath. I'm looking; Olivia's not breathing. Not breathing for 30 seconds, not breathing for a minute. After a while, her breath breaks through, as if she's getting out of the water and taking a loud gasp. Then she loses her breath again. And this kind of thing happens several times. She only goes through two breathing sessions, and she has some very interesting changes after holotropic therapy.

Literally a week later, I watched Olivia speak to a large group of students. The old emotional and behavioral effects that had to do with previous patterns of behavior were no longer evident. She was quite confident in her actions and behavior.

And it was very interesting to observe, but her external reactions, her external calibrations, and her non-verbal reactions began to resemble something related to the process of violence. She was integrating images of violence into her personality. Her nonverbal reactions began to reflect very strongly the archetypal image of the "mean girl," lashing out and sexualizing. Some lewd overtones began to appear in her actions and behavior.

In this particular case, we can observe the outcomes of integrative processes that manifest during therapeutic interventions. The associated re-experiencing of childhood images she underwent has made her more whole, albeit "different."

Subsequently observing her, we did not detect any signs of panic attacks in her behavior or public appearances.

Holotropic breathwork offers excellent opportunities for creating similar integrative processes within an individual's personality. Holotropic therapy initiates a rapid transition from one state to another. Through this process of transition, a powerful integrative process forms within our consciousness, capable of uniting various fragments of our consciousness that may have arisen in psychotraumatic situations in our lives.

For instance, when someone deeply offends you, but you manage to express your anger and disapproval regarding the event, you imprint an emotional experience, a fragmented part of yourself that will need integration and acceptance in the future. Through the expression of suppressed emotions, we can integrate the acquired experience and become more whole.

Any emotional trauma fragments our consciousness, and the sense of fragmentation actively manifests during abrupt transitions from one state to another, which we can observe in the process of holotropic breathwork.

In the mid-1960s, Stanislav Grof and his wife, Christina Grof, began actively employing this method. To this day, they assert that over their extensive 30-year journey in therapy, they have guided approximately thirty thousand individuals through this process. They report receiving a significant amount of intriguing feedback from their patients about the healing impact and effect of holotropic therapy on human consciousness.

During the exploration of these states, Stan Grof formulated a particularly interesting model that he named the "perinatal matrices of consciousness" model.

This model describes the fundamental segments of the imprints of experiences that we acquire while still in the mother's womb. These imprints were not the focus of attention or analysis in other forms of therapy. Only one of Sigmund Freud's disciples, Otto Rank, who developed ideas about birth trauma, suggested that the imprinting of the birth process could be the root of neurotic processes in a person's personality. However, Rank did not create any practices to reactivate suppressions related to this experience.

Another of Freud's disciples, Wilhelm Reich, the creator of vegetoanalysis and, to some extent, the precursor of various branches of body psychotherapy, worked with breathing techniques that allowed for the release of certain bodily suppressions. However, Reich's practices did not emphasize either the trauma of birth or the perinatal experience.

Grof asserts that the primary and fundamental traumas are not formed during childhood but even before birth, during our time in the mother's womb. Grof points out that even before birth, we live a rich emotional life that can include both positive and negative imprints. These imprints are capable of significantly influencing various factors in our emotional and behavioral dynamics as we mature into adulthood.

Grof states that there are four primary stages through which a baby passes while in the womb. He names them the first perinatal matrix, the second, third, and fourth. By organizing them in this manner, he speaks of certain essential periods, stages, or phases in the development of consciousness and personality.

The first perinatal matrix is the state of being in the womb when the embryo, still connected by the umbilical cord to the maternal bloodstream, experiences comfort, a sense of well-being, and an attachment to something greater. Grof often says that a person recalling this state experiences a sense of belonging to something much larger and more nurturing. They may have visions related to being in open space, being in very soft, comfortable places, or experiencing elements of religious visions such as being in paradise, unity with the universe, dissolution in space, or oceanic bliss.

Through the exploration of the first perinatal matrix, Grof concludes that the overwhelming majority of religions that describe states like paradise, Eden, or some other very beautiful place where people go after death typically describe the state of the first perinatal matrix, which seems to reflect the archetype of this state. Consider that Adam and Eve were in the Garden of Eden; they walked around naked and had plenty of food, warmth, and sexual pleasures. After a while, a serpent came to Adam and Eve, tempting them to eat the forbidden fruit. Following this event, Adam and Eve were banished from paradise, where they must now live in suffering. The metaphor of being banished from paradise corresponds to the infant's exit from the womb.

To some extent, the time spent in the maternal womb is like a mix of constant eating, sexual satisfaction, and material comfort. Many religions operate with the motif of expelling some of the first people from a very comfortable, pleasant place. The process of expulsion itself represents the second perinatal matrix, which occurs when the pregnant woman's placenta tears away from the fetus, causing the amniotic fluid to start draining, but the birth canal is not fully open, and the actual process of exiting the womb has not yet occurred.

The child feels that their old world is collapsing. Grof refers to this period as the second perinatal matrix, which is usually experienced as a sense of hell—an attack by evil, dark, demonic forces.

People who actively perceive these experiences, visions, and sensations often describe feeling as if they are being tortured, crushed, torn to shreds, or compressed. They experience unimaginable anguish and discomfort. The old world is crumbling, and the new one has not yet arrived, leaving the child in a very unpleasant state.

The next perinatal matrix is the matrix of exiting the womb through the birth canal, which is the third perinatal matrix. What happens to the child when they are being pushed through the mother's birth canal is an extremely intense compression.

The compression that occurs during the passage through the birth canal is typically perceived by an individual as a strong and aggressive influence on them. However, at this stage, unlike the second perinatal matrix, there is a motive of struggle and active interaction with the pressing force, on which the baby can take certain actions. This eliminates the feeling of helplessness and can create a sense of participation in combat actions.

When recalling the experience of this matrix during holotropic breathing, certain mythological images and scenes of battling monsters or adversaries with terrifying strength, like octopuses, devouring dragons, or anything trying to capture, seize, or consume, may be reproduced.

The overwhelming majority of mythological sources that depict the main heroes being devoured by dragons, snakes, or other creatures reflect states characteristic of the third perinatal matrix, containing the origins of such experiences.

According to Grof, the fourth perinatal matrix occurs when the baby experiences a sense of liberation from the pressure of the birth canal and continues for approximately the first five hours after birth, although this period of time is somewhat arbitrary.

During the passage of this matrix, a child may experience a sense of freedom, flight, or floating. Grof suggests that during this matrix, people may re-experience a sense of belonging to a global celebration, a global carnival, and global environmental changes, significantly expanding the surrounding space, as well as visions of a procession of a large number of people laughing, rejoicing, and having fun. It can be overflowing with a sense of strength, power, and energy. The dominant feeling is one of freedom and the expansion of boundaries.

Grof developed this cartography, dividing the perinatal realm into four primary matrices based on extensive feedback from patients who underwent LSD therapy at the clinic and later from participants in his holotropic breathwork seminars.

Naturally, these matrices are continually and regularly reproduced in a person's life. When we feel that everything is going well in our lives—that everything is stable, surrounded by pleasant people, living in a comfortable place, having a good job, and enjoying delicious food—we experience this state as akin to being in the womb, when everything is fine, ideal, and comfortable.

Sooner or later, every individual experiences a sense that everything seems fine, but there's a feeling that something will happen very soon. Later in a person's life, something inevitably occurs that disrupts the natural balance of the well-being they are currently experiencing. After some time, something starts to crumble, and elements of active interaction with the external world emerge, often involving struggle and resistance.

Something happens, and it may seem to the person that an overpowering force is pressing upon them—something much stronger and greater than themselves. This could manifest as issues at work, in the family, divorce, transitioning from one job to another, or an active struggle for physical survival—all of which represent the third perinatal matrix.

The fourth perinatal matrix occurs when a person emerges from these trials. It's a state of uncertainty where the old has ended, but the new has not yet fully arrived or manifested; thus, it remains undefined and ephemeral.

In our lives, we continually traverse all four perinatal matrices. For instance, when we leave daycare and enter school, when we move from school to university, when we leave university and enter the workforce, when we get married and start a family, when children are born, or when various other radical changes occur. The cyclical recurrence of these matrices in our lives is inevitable and not the goal of psychotherapy. Through the cyclical re-experiencing of these matrices, there is the opportunity for the psychoemotional content to be worked through and integrated, allowing individuals to transition to higher levels of personal functioning. While some previous issues may naturally resolve themselves, new integration challenges arise with each cycle.

What other states might be part of holotropic experiences? You may encounter significant experiences from your own life, particularly traumatic ones, which serve as the initial barrier. If you have not experienced many strong, unresolved emotions in your life, you may easily pass through the personal barrier and proceed further. However, it's worth noting that, for some people, strong childhood traumas can actually become powerful factors that propel them into the depths of their unconscious.

Beyond the layer of personal experience lie the perinatal experiences we have already described in sufficient detail. At this stage, a person may actively re-experience their birth process and even assume embryonic positions. Tremors in the body, paralysis of the hands, legs, chest, jaw, or even the entire body may occur. All these phenomena manifest and actualize various suppressed emotional energies that were part of a person's muscular armor and, to some extent, influenced and conditioned the functioning of various personality structures. The release of these energies can lead to powerful transformative processes within the individual.

Some individuals go further and enter a state of transpersonal experience, which Grof refers to as the re-experiencing of past lives. This experience can be called numinous or archetypal. Many people report this—ordinary and natural feedback from a large number of individuals who have undergone holotropic breathwork.

What is this feedback? For example, a person may feel like a different personality living in a different era, having a different family, having different children, and speaking a different language. In this state, one may re-experience key events from a previous life. Often, people recall the processes of death and dying in past incarnations. These experiences are not like dreams or ordinary fantasies. They are highly energetic re-experiences that create a significant impact on our consciousness, leading to numerous insights regarding the reasons for events in our current incarnation. Events from past incarnations can be intricately linked to events in the current incarnation in a close cause-and-effect relationship.

Awareness of congruence can evoke powerful emotional responses that deeply affect a person's muscular tension structure, consequently influencing the overall psychodynamic landscape of the personality. Grof has mentioned on several occasions that, following such experiences, he observed healing from various chronic mental and physical conditions in his patients. Belief or disbelief in these phenomena is not a prerequisite for experiencing them. They simply happen to people. How a person interprets what happened to them and what kind of experience touched their consciousness is unrelated to the therapeutic process. Each individual chooses their own way of interpreting what precisely occurred and which experience affected their consciousness. In this regard, the therapist can provide specific analytical interpretations and discuss various spiritual and mythological traditions in which what the patient encountered may be part of the tradition or ethnic belief.

During therapy, a crucial criterion is the establishment of a specific contract between the therapist and the individuals participating in the seminar. What does this contract entail? I will now describe the rules for undergoing Holotropic breathwork. Some participants in the group are already familiar with these rules, while others will become acquainted with them now.

When the session itself begins, each participant should lie down on their mat, preferably on their back, deeply relax, close their eyes, and start practicing the breathing technique.

There are no rigid rules for breathing during the process. It should simply be as deep and fast as possible. During the session, each participant can independently adjust their breathing to the rhythm of the accompanying music. The breathing should be done through the mouth. I have a specific metaphor for what I consider good breathing. Imagine that at arm's length, you are holding a burning candle. Your breath should be strong enough to significantly sway the candle's flame. Weak and shallow breathing during a holotropic session may hinder the possibility of reaching truly intense emotions. By the way, the inability to breathe deeply and intensely serves as a strong criterion that a person is harboring significant psycho-emotional suppressions.

After some time, typically 10–20 minutes of intense breathing, many participants start experiencing altered states of consciousness. I observe entire choirs of various shouts, moans, cries, and wails that arise during the group. Some group participants occasionally begin to emit sounds that are rather challenging to classify as human. After the group, participants often cannot identify the reasons for the sound effects they produced, although in other cases, there could be detailed feedback describing the intense experiences being relived.

If you feel an aggressive impulse or a strong urge to vent your anger physically, such as by hitting something or someone, you are allowed to safely punch the floor or wave your arms in front of you. Everything is okay; this can be an integral part of the therapeutic process. The most important thing to remember is that somewhere nearby, there might be another person undergoing therapy. It's advisable not to harm them. I will, of course, be monitoring to ensure that you don't injure each other. In my practice, there has never been a single instance of anyone harming another person during Holotropic breathwork, so there's no need to worry on that account.

Furthermore, if you have a sensation that you want to laugh, cry, or express your emotions in any other way, allow those feelings to emerge. Any attempts to suppress the expression of various emotions during Holotropic breathwork can lead to reacting to them later after the therapeutic group, possibly in contexts that may not be particularly suitable. It's important to remember that, after experiencing emotions, seeking the assistance of a therapist may be necessary, so don't miss the opportunity to receive qualified help and support. The context of the therapeutic group is maximally adapted to healing processes, and all forms of emotional expression are highly appropriate, especially within this context.

During the breathing process, some individuals may experience active visual sensations, often in abundance. These can manifest as flashes of color and light or as diverse mystical journeys filled with powerful inner energy. People predisposed to visual representations may encounter this kind of experience frequently.

For some participants, visual representations may be minimal or absent altogether. Sensations coursing through the body might be the predominant experience. There is no need for concern in this regard. The appearance of images is not a mandatory criterion for effective therapy. Flowing images may appear during some breathing sessions and disappear during others. Our unconscious guides sensory representations during the breathing process, and obtaining precisely what one desires can be quite challenging. It's not like ordering a movie. Perception during breathing begins to shift toward areas where there are more emotional suppressions, allowing an individual to experience the release of these suppressions. Although we have encountered group participants who had very strong emotional childhood traumas, some of them managed to avoid re-experiencing the trauma during breathing and transitioned sharply into transpersonal experiences. Sometimes, a person simply needs to be ready to confront their inner demons. When they are prepared, the unconscious opens the path, and emotions begin to be realized. Until then, we may encounter direct or indirect resistance to experiencing emotional states.

Under no circumstances should you abruptly stand up during a holotropic session due to spontaneously arising desires or attempt to leave the room without the therapist's consent. This is because of the contract: once you start breathing, you continue until the end of the session. It's advisable not to leave the seminar before it concludes, as the feelings awakened within you can generate very unusual desires, such as a sudden urge to go somewhere or engage in strange activities, and so on. There have been individuals who, despite my requirements, still decided to leave, but they left in a somewhat disoriented state. Be aware that the feelings awakened during breathing can have extremely aggressive and intense focal points, so it's essential to maintain maximum control. I adhere to the framework, and I must breathe until the end of the session.

Furthermore, if the sensations in your body become too uncomfortable and, for specific reasons, you cannot breathe at all, feel extremely fatigued, and are unable to inhale and exhale, raise your hand, and I will see your raised hand. I will approach you and ask how you are doing. What can I do to help you? You might say something like, "I can't continue; I feel very unwell." I would respond by saying, "Alright, lie down quietly here; allow others to breathe peacefully, okay?" I can interrupt the holotropic breathing of a specific person if I deem it necessary and appropriate at that moment.

During the breathing session, I may approach each of you to work with your body. What does this mean? For example, if Emma's legs are actively moving, or if there's excessive sensation through the movement of her arms and head, I can come over, sit nearby, and use my hands to stabilize the areas of her body where there is excessive movement.

At the moment, if you feel that I have blocked a specific form of your movement, you should continue to act and move those limbs until the feelings of excessive impulse subside. I can block leg movements, arm movements, or head movements while instructing the individual to continue moving. Some individuals may experience full-body spasms during the session, where a person lying on their mat starts to arch their body, rising onto their neck. In such cases, I can approach that person and, by placing my hands on them, fully ground them. I've had instances where a participant in a breathing session went into a bridge position and held me up in the air for several minutes due to the intense emotional energy being released from her. Later, she descended and, with sudden spontaneous impulses, lifted me upward.

Grof has mentioned that in his practice, some patients have maintained the bridge position for up to 45 minutes. Here, we're talking about the sensation of experiencing unusual feelings. The key is to keep breathing until the end of the session while the music is playing. After the session ends, I lower the music volume and slowly instruct you to conclude your breathing, after which you should lie on your mats for a while. Do not get up abruptly, as it can lead to severe dizziness. It's better to rest for 2–5 minutes after the breathing session.

I'll mention that at this point, you can stop breathing, and you do so. Once you've recovered, we will reconvene in a circle and begin sharing the feelings we experienced during the session, providing feedback on the experience if you feel the need. However, more often than not, participants want to share.

After some time, you'll lie down again, and we'll begin working again. Today, there will be two breathing sessions, and tomorrow, there will be two more. Some people may experience interesting, unusual sensations in the first session, while others may experience them in the fourth session, and some may not experience them at all during this holotropic seminar. It's important to understand that we are all different, and psychodynamic processes occur differently for each of us. It's possible that breakthroughs to new and interesting states occur after a series of seminars, but I encounter this very rarely.

I also want to point out that it's preferable not to engage in excessively aggressive actions or activities that may cause harm to other participants between the two breathing sessions. Avoid alcohol and drugs during the breaks between today and tomorrow. During these intervals, it's advisable to abstain from heavy foods and to opt for light meals, herbal tea, and refraining from sexual contact. Experiencing intense sensations is possible, but excessive release of emotional sexual energy can lead to very negative states afterward. Also, sexual activity may deprive you of the necessary level of awareness, which is one of the main goals of participating in a psychotherapeutic group. So, let's adhere to the regulations, gentlemen.

Furthermore, after the entire holotropic breathing seminar, certain recommendations apply. For a minimum of a week, avoid making any significant life decisions for yourself and your loved ones. The emotions touched upon during the seminar need time to settle and integrate. Only after that will your decisions be maximally appropriate for the life context to which you belong. These are elementary precautions. It would be incorrect to say that after the holotropic breathing seminar, you will be obsessed with strange ideas about reforming your life; this occurs relatively rarely. Nevertheless, as a precaution, it's worth taking basic measures that can protect you from unpleasant and inappropriate situations in your life.

For some people, emotional reactions after the seminar may manifest as vivid and abundant dreams. Some participants may experience insomnia. These phenomena are temporary and should not be a cause for concern. Simply allow your emotions to naturally emerge from within you and create a new, more complete, and harmonious state within you.

Alright, these are the basic guidelines. Any questions?

Participant: Will there be any additional emotional suppressions created by the restrictions after holotropic breathing?

Therapist: Look, here we're talking about social norms that you should still adhere to at a basic level and safety rules primarily oriented toward your well-being. Sometimes, inappropriate, uncontrolled emotional reactions can lead to quite a few problems. One of my psychotherapist colleagues once told me a story about a case with one of her patients. To allow her patients to release pent-up anger, she often used Alexander Lowen's techniques of body therapy. In her office, she kept a large number of plastic cups that she would give to her patients to break if she noticed emotional aggression in them. In working with one patient, she used up more than a hundred cups. Initially, he would break them with his hands. Then she started worrying that he was injuring his hands, so she began placing these cups on the floor for him to stomp on. Thus, their therapy session revolved around destroying entirely innocent plastic cups. However, it seems that during the session itself, they never quite reached the root source of the emotional suppression. The patient left after the session, and when he came for the next one, he reported that he had gotten into a fight at the bus station right after the therapy session. This is an example of what you should avoid. I'm not saying that you will necessarily have a similar experience, but minimal safety boundaries serve therapy and the preservation of your mental health.

Participant: I've already been to two holotropic breathing sessions, and I experience spasms in my face, and I get the urge to close my mouth. I expend a lot of energy to keep my mouth open.

Therapist: Does your jaw spasm?

Participant: Yes, it becomes uncontrollable.

Therapist: Look, I had a patient in his thirties, a former priest who decided to study psychology and became my student. Once, during holotropic breathing, his chest and jaw completely spasmed, and I had to approach him and give a massage to release the contracted muscles. I started rhythmically pressing on his chest and unclenching his jaw; he couldn't breathe, and he lay there gasping for air. What happens when our chest and jaw spasm like this? It's a manifestation of repressed anger, which, for some reason, we can't fully express at that moment. Typically, such suppressions are present in individuals with strong moral constraints. What should you do when this spasm occurs? Try to focus on your breathing, no matter what happens. The key is to keep breathing, and sooner or later, the blockage will clear, and you'll feel better. Your body will find a way to express the emotions hidden behind your emotional tightness. Sometimes, a person simply fears breathing too deeply. There might be an unconscious fear of fully revealing the emotional component that lies deep within our consciousness. You shouldn't rush or delay. If there is a need to move around on your mat during the session, feel free to do so. You can try changing positions, curling up in a fetal position, or, if necessary, even lying on your stomach. However, in my opinion, lying on your stomach is one of the worst positions for holotropic breathing, as it severely restricts a full breathing cycle. The optimal position is lying on your back. But, alas, not all participants can maintain a supine position for an extended period, especially those accustomed to sleeping on their sides or stomachs. Nonetheless, there are no strict or rigid rules regarding placement.

Some participants in the process of holotropic work may

be very mobile. They may try to crawl away or move somewhere during the breathing process. This pattern is especially characteristic of people who are involved in sports, martial arts, or dancing; that is, people who are used to expressing their emotions through motor kinesthetics. For one participant in the group, I remember we had to lay several mats down because, when she started to breathe, she was constantly rolling in different directions. In doing so, her rolls could look a lot like strange dances on the floor. Once, while she was breathing, she crawled up to the wall and began to climb up on top of it with her legs. There was a lot of sexual, unexpressed feeling in her movements. When she was given feedback regarding her lived experience, she commented that she realized she was a prostitute on a pirate ship on which she was having group sex with the pirates. Her personal history included early childhood sexual abuse. When she was five years old, she was molested by a twelve-year-old boy. She met with him for several days in a row and, as she reported, engaged in various forms of sex. She didn't remember being forced; there was no literal violence there. She even commented that she loved what she was experiencing at the time. But alas, this childhood sexual experience had consequences for her; she was unable to have a meaningful sexual relationship with any man until she was twenty-one. The problem was that every time she had an affair and she and her partner were already in bed, she would have a panic attack, quickly get dressed, and run away. In this way, she ended relationships with over ten partners. It took me over three months of individual therapy to correct this state of affairs. After therapy, she was able to find a man and still have sex with him, even though the relationship was quite short-lived. The Holotropic Breathing sessions she participated in were, in many ways, symbolic and grotesque reflections of her childhood experiences of sexual interaction. In this case, we can observe that the compensatory defense mechanisms of the psyche that are characteristic of the dream world may be activated during the process of holotropic breathing. That is, she was not literally experiencing sexual interaction in her childhood; the unconscious was constructing a specific plot for her, reflecting her childhood experience. Thus, we can look at this case from a more classical psychoanalytic point of view. If we go into the transpersonal zone of interpretation, then we can make the assumption that she may have been connecting to the experience of her past incarnation in the process of breathing, and that what happened to her as a child was a kind of echo of these experiences. But for therapy, ways of interpretation are tools. The interpretation that is chosen can be the key to the most optimal transformative processes that can be achieved in working with the patient. In this case, we can recall a quote from Milton Erickson, who said that "... psychotherapy cannot afford to have rigid interpretations of reality."

Feedback: Commencement of Breathwork

Therapist: Ladies and gentlemen, how do you feel before the breathwork session? Please provide brief feedback.

Emma: Right now, I feel calm. I'm slightly concerned about my health, and I want to go through all of this. But overall, I'm fine. I had a little backache when I lay down.

Sophia: I guess I'm anxious. I don't know what to expect because everything is unknown to me.

Amelia: This isn't my first session. I hope there will be something new. I sense there's unrealized emotional potential inside, so I'm ready to work.

Isabella: What am I expecting? I want to change my life. I hope to consider this the next step in changing my life.

Ava: Right now, I'm concerned about whether I can breathe normally because my jaw is clenched and I have a swollen tooth. I'm worried if I'll be able to breathe properly. Apart from that, everything's fine.

Peter: I want to free myself from the unprocessed moments of life and the emotions associated with them. Those emotions hinder me from moving forward.

Olivia: My goal is to work on the fear of death.

James: Expectations for this immersion: it's a release of aggression, anxiety, and an accumulation of energy.

Luna: I hope the journey will be good, and I'll enjoy it. Well, if it turns out to be a challenging journey, then I'll gladly watch it.

Mia: Getting rid of complexes.

Amelia: I want to refine the feelings that caused discomfort and misunderstanding in the previous session. I hope to work on this and get rid of those feelings.

Charlotte: I have many expectations: releasing aggression, dealing with suppressed emotions, and embracing something new. There are many expectations, but it seems to me that there's no specific outline.

Therapist: So, I think we should get down to practice.

Feedback: First Breathwork Session

Isabella: I experienced a terrible spasm around my clavicle and neck that made it impossible for me to breathe or do anything. My entire body was incredibly tense. I felt the urge to cry, but due to my breathing, I couldn't. Then it burst out, and I cried a little. But in general, it felt like I was being choked; I could clearly feel it. I couldn't inhale. My entire body was extremely tense. I couldn't relax at all. My back was burning and hurting terribly—just awful pain.

Therapist: Muscle tensions are being released, and it can be very painful.

Isabella: What's causing the tension here?

Therapist: The clavicle and neck represent ego tension. These muscles tense up when we excessively focus on ourselves. When we are more attuned to the world, these muscles relax. Too much fixation on the ego and too little on the world. The extensive pain radiating through the back indicates that the ego has experienced many different emotionally traumatic experiences, which you still have to confront.

Peter: It was interesting when relaxation began. After all the convulsions, there was a complete absence of time and space perception. A new, unfamiliar space, and being present in it. This space was simultaneously dark and light, but not very pleasant, although I wanted to stay there. It was brief. There was also a sense of déjà vu, as if something like this had happened to me before and these feelings had already been experienced.

Sophia: It was great, but my body occasionally went into spasms. I had a smile that I couldn't control. Sensation-wise, there was coldness in my hands and constant, uncontrollable body movements. Right now, there's a feeling of joy.

Emma: Initially, there were few images. Most of the sensations were in my body. It all began with wings growing on me. Then, I felt like I was transported to different eras. Then, I distinctly remember being a mermaid because it felt like my legs were sewn together, forming a fin. It was quite horrifying; I couldn't move. Then, there were only sensations in my body, as if it were some wandering energy. It would go into my arms, then my legs, and both would experience tremors. Later, the vibration in my limbs moved into my body, and I began to arch. There were very few images—practically none. In the beginning, just a few. Toward the end, some sort of groan came out of me, I think. Music somehow contributed to this auditory expression. Well, there were plenty of sensations in my body, many unfamiliar ones.

Olivia: Images of people from a primitive communal time appeared immediately. I lived through several lives of different individuals (mostly male), specifically the process of their dying: one was torn apart by a bear, another by a boar, bitten by a snake, touched a poisonous flower, and perished in battle with other natives. Then, I relived the same events, but now I had knowledge of how to handle such situations, and I had gained greater strength and agility. I defeated both the bear and the adversaries practically with my bare hands, the snake, and so on. I knew what was poisonous and what wasn't. There was knowledge about everything needed for survival in the world. Then, I realized I had shifted to the Incas: their ordinary life—hunting, daily existence... I see myself dying (apparently as a man, a sage) with no strength left, but I'm calm. They open my veins to ease the passing. Then, they cut open my belly and fill it with aromatic herbs. I'm at ease with this; I wasn't afraid to die. My life was lived with purpose. The next incarnation is in the same place. I see the sails of Spanish and Portuguese ships. I understand they are invaders. I feel hatred toward them. At the same time, I am one of the sailors, looking at new land and anticipating how we'll enslave the indigenous people and bring wealth to my family in Europe. There was a battle; many died, and all the invaders perished. After several more years, the tribes lived in peace, but ships came again, even more invaders, better armed. They exterminated the indigenous people, cruelly torturing, crucifying, and burning them in huts. Catholic churches were built everywhere. Then there were several incarnations in different parts of the world—Africa, India. Initially, societies lived by their own laws, in harmony with nature—not always entirely well, but harmoniously. Then, "white people" arrived with their customs and began to restrict, exploit, and exterminate the local population. Hunger, disease, prisons, and disillusionment befell them. Society gradually developed; multi-story buildings appeared, more and more of them, until there were skyscrapers everywhere. People who felt nature's rhythms gradually disappeared into reservations. At some point, I'm walking through the streets—only towering skyscrapers, asphalt, and concrete. It's horrifying. I see no one else and hear nothing—only an artificial stone world around me. Then, I am the planet Earth—these stone jungles suffocate it; there are almost no trees or living nature left in the world. It decides to cleanse itself of all this, causing some catastrophe. Almost all the people perished; only a few survivors remain. I searched for them. I am a man, walking through the snow; endless snow stretches around, and nothing else, just silence, only the wind. Occasionally, I encounter some wildlife, such as seals, hares, and wolves, but that's not frightening. In the cities, among people, it was scarier. I eat raw fish and any small animal I can catch. Then, I encounter a polar bear and then a mammoth. I say goodbye to my companions, climb onto the mammoth's back, and, burying myself in its fur, doze off or gaze at the stars. Finally, the mammoth brings me to the tribe. I'm welcomed. These are the people who managed to survive after the catastrophe. Due to their state, they barely remember their previous lives and live rather simply. I find myself a wife; we have children. Then, I live to old age, observing how the tribe develops. I'm a respected person because I arrived from afar and remember better what was before.

Ava: The first thing that happened was people— butterflies living in flowers. Then there were snakes with precious stone bracelets, like collars with three stone bracelets. Next was a living fish skeleton. There's a head and a tail skeleton, but it swims in the water as if nothing's happened. There was a crocodile with daggers instead of ridges. Then a lot of little people— dwarves— carried a big wooden pipe. The next image was a fox with a rainbow tail. It had a tail like a rainbow. Next was an image of an Asian corpse shot in the head, with a little pool of blood next to it, flowing from the head. Then an asteroid approached Earth. Initially, it was a beautiful picture: space, stars; then, as the camera switched, a massive asteroid flew toward Earth. Then there was a hand controlling the movement of spiders. A huge hand, rays emanating from the fingers, and the spiders moved, following the hand's motion. After that, there were schematic little people jumping off a cliff. Soon, an interpretation came to me, as if these were the deceased who couldn't move on, and they eternally jumped off the cliff. That's why they were schematic— because they no longer existed among the living. Next were armored battle rays and pterodactyls. And then I stopped breathing, but the images kept coming. It was a half-cow, half-elk, meaning one part was a cow and the next part was an elk. Then a cat moved to the rhythm of music, but then it started breaking into pieces: the head and the ears separately, as if someone had cut a fish into pieces. It was the same with the cat, but at the same time, it continued to dance to the rhythm of the music. Then Cherokee Indians collected stones from the sky. And finally, the haircut of a big head with a lawnmower.

Therapist: The images you experienced are very diverse, stream-like, and fantastical. In this case, it can be said that your large cerebral hemispheres' activity has almost entirely given way to your subcortical structures, which "joyfully" began to share with you the accumulated phylogenetic experience—something that is likely a deep genetic imprint and can, in certain life moments, be released, manifested, and understood. This can also be referred to as an entry into the deep transpersonal experience. Many of the images you went through possess archetypal significance and arise from different cultures. Stanislav Grof commented that a person experiencing such an experience can sometimes produce archetypal images that they have never seen, heard, or read about. For example, there was one case where a seminar participant, during Holotropic breathwork, began to realize they were hovering in the northern lights. Later, Grof discovered that the Chukchi people believe that paradise is located precisely there, and "good" souls, after death, hover in the northern lights. Many examples of cross-cultural memories have been accumulated, so such phenomena are not isolated.

Amelia: Today it was less vivid and not as consistent as I am used to experiencing. In the beginning, there was just an image of a she-wolf. I saw her; or it was me; or I was just looking at her. There was a she-wolf, and then this image went away. Then there was a hare, and I thought it was the hare from "Alice in Wonderland," and I should see something, or he should show me something. I followed him; he went somewhere in the thicket. I was walking, walking, walking somewhere, and something there was scary. Then a big spider appeared, but overall, it was normal and calm. Then I was taken by aliens, either for research or for the exchange of experience. Some time ago, I was on a spaceship, and there was a robot. Next, I'm in Africa. I'm a boy; I'm about 12 years old, and I'm walking with a lion. And then I realize that a shaman has chosen me to teach him. I was living this boy's life, going back to childhood, then back to adolescence. I knew that I would learn a lot, but at the same time, there were many moments when, for example, children would avoid me. I was accompanied by a sense of loneliness throughout my life. Then, back, I am an adult; I have wives and children, but the feeling of loneliness does not leave me. During the training period, there was something unpleasant, like eating animals and other things. But in general, nothing was treated—people and animals— as I remember the war. I lived a very long time, and I outlived my wives and many children. I remember this shaman. He was without a face but also in feathers, rings, and tusks, but I don't remember exactly. Next, I was in a Slavic pagan culture. I was a man, and I was riding through the forest on a horse with a sword as an outpost. I remember there was war and killing people, but they were enemies. And that's exactly the difference: when I was African, I was killing whites, and when I was white, I was killing Tatar-Mongols. But it was lonely too.

Therapist: I see that many of the participants today have just experienced a boom in transpersonal experiences. This is very interesting. I think sometimes in a group there can be a resonance effect when one participant, for whatever reason, has a very deep experience, and the other participants sort of emotionally follow him into a more intense experience. But that's just an assumption.

Isabella: Initially, in the process of holotropic breathing, I started to finish all the things that were unfinished, starting from my childhood. A story from my childhood: when my uncle took me for a ride on a tractor, I fell asleep at the wheel. I couldn't really do anything at that point, and we crashed into a tree, but it was all okay. During the holotropic session, I learned how to drive the tractor. In addition to that, there were images of me riding a horse. Then, I had images of people playing musical instruments that were completely unknown to me. Also, the craziest image for me was one where I was milking cows, even though I had never done that in my life. Throughout the whole session, I had some sort of head peeking out from behind my right shoulder. Initially, I tried to chase it away, but then I told myself to let it lie there, and I would breathe through it. It was the face of someone I didn't know, and the more I breathed, the more the face became dark and lost its features. And towards the end, this face became like a ball that was next to me. I was trying to either get that ball out or hit it, and it was still lying to the right. I wish I could have worked something out in the next session. In the drawing, I reflected the main images: the ball, the musical instruments, the cows, and the gearbox in the tractor (laughs).

Therapist: Milking a cow is a peak transpersonal experience, the most archetypal (the group laughs).

Nikolai: My breath kept stopping again and again. There was a peculiar breath-blocking phenomenon, but at the same time, there were intense bodily sensations. My body was trembling, my arms were numb up to the elbows, and my legs were numb up to the knees. I tried to think about someone, but my anxiety level prevented me from focusing on anything personal. In my thoughts, I was in Maidan (Kyiv, Ukraine), in Crimea, in Kharkov. My drawing simultaneously represents the tents on Maidan and the ships in the Black Sea. Well, right now, I'm in a very trance-like state. I can note that in previous holotropic sessions, my jaw was clenched tightly, but now it was unrealistically heavy.

Luna: My drawing is a symbol of harmony. As for sensations, there was a strong dryness in my mouth and control over my breath. There was also movement in my legs and body that helped me breathe. There were no images at all. In addition to the sensations, there were also spasms in the body that went towards the solar plexus.

Evelyn: Initially, the image of the sea came, as if I were living on some island. I experienced a large number of tactile sensations: touching the sand, swimming in the water with dolphins. Then came ordinary life. I felt a sense of danger related to the presence of some kind of anaconda snake. I knew I was strong, but this feeling didn't leave me. Nevertheless, I encountered this snake, and we started to fight. During this struggle, it strangled and swallowed me; my death occurred inside this snake. The next transition was to the northern regions, where I was a hunter who was eaten by wolves. I felt the pain that was tearing me apart. Next was an image where I found myself in some abandoned industrial complex alone. I walked there and got into a pipe from which I couldn't get out. As a result, there was a feeling of being confined and doomed. Nevertheless, I managed to get out of this pipe and found myself in this abandoned factory. Everything around me was gloomy and gray, but suddenly I noticed a certain flower that resembled a seven-petal flower. It was a magical flower that grants wishes. I plucked a petal and made a wish to get out of this world. After a few seconds, I ended up in another world where there was green vegetation and beautiful nature. Everything was wonderful there, very calm, but there were no people there either. There were animals, and I could breathe well, but the feeling of loneliness suffocated me. I simply walked and ended up near a waterfall, and at that moment, I thought that I should commit suicide. However, I realized that it was foolish and chose to stay alive by the waterfall. Next, I was somehow found by a little bear cub, with which I lived. Also, my left hand worried me; it felt mechanical, and there was a brand on it. I was afraid that I could turn into a robot. The next image was that I was lying down, and in front of me was a small gray spider. I had a feeling of disgust and fear. I thought that I was tired of living like this and suffering. I provoked the spider, and it bit me. I lay down, and my soul split in two: one part hovered above the ground, and the other was on the ground. There was a feeling of inevitability because the spiders wove a web around me and were going to feast on me. At some point, I became weightless and flew away. I became nothing, some sort of essence, and from this, I was simply happy that I was not a human or even a living being. Then I flew into space and became a kind of cosmic dust that floated among the stars. Next, I found myself on Mars, from where I saw Earth. I understood that Mars was my first homeland, and Earth was the second. I felt good there, but I missed Earth. Suddenly, I saw how Earth collided with a comet, and there was a feeling that there was nothing left on it—complete emptiness. The next image was that I flew to another planet; it was blue and lifeless. I was overcome by a sense of doom because I couldn't even die here. Calming down, I began to awaken life here, on this planet. There, I began to realize that I was no longer a robot. I was very happy that there were no spiders on this planet. After some time, water began to appear, and life began to sprout. Flowers grew, and I was glad that I had brought something here. Then, towards the end of my journey, I realized that my time had come. I lay down, realizing that I had done everything I could, and trees sprouted through me as a symbol of something new in this world.

Charlotte: The first image was that of a colossal snake crawling between rocks. Everything around was ablaze—more than just a fire—and this snake was attempting to escape the flames, but it grew furious with itself for its inability to do so. Moreover, there were numerous snakes around her, attacking her and causing her to flee. Despite the fact that these other snakes couldn't harm her in reality, nevertheless, the snake burned in the fire, and tranquility followed. Then, another image emerged: a white table and a war between the USA and some other country. There was someone at the head, and people surrounded him, seemingly just for numbers. One phrase persisted throughout this vision: "We will eliminate them." I do not know who was eliminating whom, but this phrase echoed with strain, as if it were a challenge. There was also a great deal of various weapons firing from all directions. As for bodily sensations, my hands were completely numb, and I would alternately feel intense heat and coldness.

Day One: Lecture Two

What happens when we breathe very deeply? What exactly occurs within our physiology when we engage in hyperventilation of the lungs? What effects does it produce? Paradoxically, the more intense our breathing, the more our cerebral blood vessels tend to spasm, causing blood that was abundantly circulating in the cortex of the large hemispheres to shift towards our subcortex, the repository of our phylogenetic experience, some of which certain participants actively encountered during the last session. The functioning of the cortex of the large hemispheres is closely linked to the overall muscular tension in the body. Therefore, individuals with more muscular blocks may find it more difficult to release themselves into a deep and complete journey through the realms of our unconscious. From my experience, I have often observed that participants who are deeply engrossed in cognitive processes and who engage in excessive thinking and contemplation in their daily lives may have greater challenges achieving profound relaxation and entering deep trance states. This is due to the hypertrophic development of the left hemisphere of the brain, where language and cognitive centers reside.

Individuals who introduce sports and art into their lives are more adept at releasing muscular tensions, and they tend to feel more at ease in Holotropic breathwork sessions. This could be associated with the greater activity of the right hemisphere, which, unlike the left, operates more effortlessly with abstract ideas, perceives time non-linearly, and is capable of simultaneously recreating numerous processes in consciousness.

People with significantly active right hemispheres usually quickly and easily experience peak states in Holotropic breathwork sessions, characterized by their transpersonal and archetypal splendor.

We will indicate **four levels of holotropic experience**:

- **Level 0**: During the Holotropic breathwork session, no significantly distinguishable effects are observed. Some vague bodily sensations may arise.
- **Level 1**: Noticeable changes in bodily sensations are present, accompanied by some trance-like experiences; although they are low in intensity and do not lead to significant changes or transformative experiences.
- **Level 2**: Strong and noticeable transformational processes occur within consciousness. Various sensory experiences manifest.
- **Level 3**: The holotropic experience is vivid and impressive. There is an abundance of diverse sensations. Transpersonal experiences are present, leading to profound and meaningful changes in one's personality.
- **Level 4**: This is a unique experience similar to the third level, but in this case, something extraordinary occurs. Realization of this can significantly and radically alter a person's life, their behavior, and their understanding of the world and themselves.

During the temporary inhibition of the activity of the large hemispheres' cortex, our psyche's defense mechanisms temporarily slow down, gradually ceasing to trouble us with our everyday life problems. During this time, deeply suppressed fragments of experience, which have always been with us on one level but remained inactive and unexpressed due to their lack of involvement in our basic social routine, are granted the opportunity to break through into our consciousness.

For some individuals, the emotional release from the hypercontrol of the activity of the hemispheres' cortex happens rapidly. For others, it occurs very gradually. For instance, in Ava's case, this process occurs almost instantaneously. After just ten minutes of breathing, she experienced abundant visual hallucinations and illusions. In contrast, for other participants, this process can be very smooth and gradual. For the third group, the cortex of the large hemispheres can maintain its tight control for a very extended period, preventing the individual from fully delving into their inner self even after many Holotropic breathwork sessions in succession. I have witnessed such cases; though in my observations, they are relatively rare.

What we encounter in the depths of our unconscious, where our phylogenetic experience is concentrated, Carl Jung referred to as the "collective unconscious." It represents a particular concentration of experience containing various mythical images—archetypes. According to Jung, these archetypes are the "atoms" of consciousness, guiding our personalities at high abstract levels and largely predetermining the life paths we follow.

Feedback: Second Breathwork Session

Olivia: Vivid and intensely colorful images appeared during the session, unlike anything I've ever seen before. I found myself in what seemed like an Indian palace, touching the rough stones on its walls. In front of me was a bright yellow chick with delicate down, while the elephant's skin felt dry and rough to my touch. I could see beautiful flowers and feel their cool freshness. I interacted with all these elements, touching them and experiencing their textures. Later, various activities unfolded: crafting weapons, molding clay pitchers, and more. It went on for a while, and everything was beautiful. However, my real body became extremely cold, causing discomfort. My head was hot, while my legs felt icy. I wanted to understand the meaning behind these sensations and began to think that I might be a sperm cell. All my energy seemed concentrated in my head, and my legs felt like a tail.

I saw an egg cell in front of me, and I witnessed fertilization. I observed the gradual division and development of the egg cell. I could vividly see the formation of an embryo, passing through stages of evolutionary development. I knew what this person would become—I saw them as a child, then as an 18-year-old girl, beautiful, active, cheerful, and intelligent. Everything seemed to be shaping up exceptionally well and successfully in all aspects of her life. But suddenly, for an unclear reason, the process of egg cell development halted, freezing at the lizard stage, just before the image of the child emerged. I either lost the image or fell asleep, but something had clearly gone wrong. I started feeling uncertain and fearful. Everything disappeared, and for a while, I couldn't see anything. Then, a large (probably about a meter in size) gray, furry spider approached me, standing over me and staring at me. I felt terrified, turned to the other side, and then saw only black and white, frightening images—an empty bucket, the silhouette (shadow) of a cat, and something else—all unsettling, incomprehensible, and scary. This marked the end of the second session.

Therapist: I believe what you experienced represents a symbolic transition from the first basic perinatal matrix to the second. This is often how it unfolds. The sensation of a pleasant, favorable flow of circumstances, a feeling of a bright future, and wonderful prospects is usually followed by various furry spiders that disrupt the entire picture of a positive transpersonal experience. It's important to understand that we are dealing more with an imprint of an experience than a literal one, and this imprint exists in every individual to some degree. During the breathing process, we navigate through these imprints. If you find yourself stuck in this particular experience right now, there's nothing to worry about. In the next breathing session, the dynamics will actualize once again, and you will be able to move forward. There's no need to be concerned about it; simply accept the experience as it manifests in this session.

Ava: I had a very intense journey, and there were many more images than I've ever experienced before. It was such a challenging session, and it started normally but then turned into a nightmare. First, there was a cross descending into a cross-shaped wormwood, and you could see it going down until it was at the bottom in the water, and then the wormwood closed up. The second part was the removal of pagan crosses and symbols and their replacement with Christian crosses. Then, I saw myself as a she-wolf fighting with dogs and protecting her wolf cubs. Next, there was an abandoned building, and as I walked deeper into it, there was a hall with a throne-like chair, and sitting on the throne was a skeleton wearing royal clothing. Then there was a beetle-scarab that froze everything it touched. After that, I saw the devil's finger—a natural phenomenon where water begins to freeze into a column, and this ice freezes everything on the bottom that couldn't escape. Next was a dog-armor-bearer, like it was walking above me from below. It looked like a dog, but it had scales like an armadillo on its belly.

Then there was an image of a skunk, but instead of the typical odor, it emitted pine cones. Following that, I found myself under the ice. There was a shaman standing above me, and he was melting the ice. As the ice melted, I began to awaken. I felt like I was something ancient, and I was being awakened. Next, I saw myself as a young woman fighting, holding a shield with Celtic ornaments in one hand and a hammer in the other. In the next image, I was trapped in a snow globe. It was an actual New Year's souvenir, and it was very cold. I was wearing a linen dress that went all the way to the floor. Then, there was an antique camera with a separate flash, but instead of a flash, chocolate candies were falling out. After that, there was a mummified hand playing on ribs, and following that, there was a spider descending on a small web, and as it descended, it grew in size. When it reached the ground, it transformed into a person wearing a black hooded cloak with a cross drawn on the back of the cloak. The next image was a grasshopper with laser eyes that burned everything in its path.

Then there was a wooden house with a porch, and as I stepped onto the porch, it elongated and turned into a kind of bridge that floated above the ground. Next, there was a negative image: people dancing around a bonfire where a person was being cooked. Then there were whales, dolphins, and fish being washed ashore. At this point, I felt really unwell because I love mice and rats. There was a store window with mousetraps and rat traps where rats and mice were hanging, and they were selling poison, etc. Next was Carlson-Frankenstein, a stitched-together person with a huge propeller on their back. They could fly, but they were very eerie, with metallic fangs. I don't like the color pink, but I found myself in a pink room wearing a pink straitjacket, which was a nightmare for me, and I couldn't do anything about it. After that, there was a bridge with people on it, which collapsed into a turbulent mountain river. And finally, there was a group—a herd of fighting goats and animals—that were killing each other in this brawl, and there were no survivors.

Therapist: You experienced almost pure poetry in the second perinatal matrix—vivid and colorful representations of this sphere. If we consider them through the lens of perinatal philosophy, they are the products of a sense of interruption of the blissful state of the first perinatal matrix. Our perceptual apparatus begins to construct various decorations to convey the full dramatic nature of this experience. A close friend of Stanislav Grof, Swiss artist H.R. Giger predominantly painted his works in the style of the second perinatal matrix. In the late 1970s, he worked as a set decorator on the film "Alien" with Sigourney Weaver. He created the image of the "Alien" itself, a horrifying monster from another planet that implants its offspring in the bodies of human colonists. Giger succeeded in creating this image with great quality and completeness; he received an Oscar for his work as a set decorator. When a creative individual manages to attune to the emotional energies of any perinatal matrix, what emerges in the creative process can astonish and deeply affect other people, since such an experience is an integral part of our consciousness and psyche.

Amelia: I felt very well. Firstly, I was a girl, finally. I was overjoyed by this. At the beginning, an image of a unicorn with a beautiful, silvery, and iridescent horn came to mind—a beautiful white horse. I was a girl, around 18 years old, wearing a long white sundress like they did in medieval times. Then our settlement was attacked. I saw houses burning, as if it were a raid by nomads—Turks or Tatars. They took us captive and brought us somewhere. It felt like Turkey, and we were enslaved. They took men and women, but women were used as servants and men for various violent games and battles. I lived and worked there, but I don't remember much violence. The only thing is that it was difficult and humiliating. Eventually, I killed my owner by cutting his throat and escaped. For a long time, I walked through the sands. I remember the burning sand and the lack of water. I arrived at the sea, and there, a fisherman appeared. After some time, we started living together, and I realized he was my husband. We lived together, and we had children: a girl and a boy. When the children grew up, a unicorn came to me again and took me to some fantastical land. I don't remember what was there, but there were fantastical images of animals. Then, I learned something, and I returned, and my family understood that I was absent, and they were understanding about it. I realized that I possessed supernatural knowledge. I stayed with them, but periodically, I could go into meditation, into another reality, and there, through dances and wearing different dresses, I gained knowledge. Besides that, I was there, in reality, by the shore, engaging in some sword fighting for concentration and training. Later, my family started to have abilities, and we swam a lot. We could swim underwater like amphibians. The children could communicate with animals. For a long time, we lived here by the shore, and then we started traveling. It appeared that we were transported to all the places on our planet, sharing experiences. Then, a space journey began, and we were on all the planets in the solar system. There was no one on some planets, but on Saturn, we definitely communicated with someone. Then, we got sucked into a black hole that transformed me and my whole family into atoms and particles. On one hand, the Universe is composed of me, and at the same time, I am a part of this Universe. Such a state: I'm everywhere and nowhere. Then, we transformed back and returned home, where we lived. Later, I realized that I was sitting by the shore and pregnant; I would have a child, and there was such harmony around. Again, a unicorn came, and everything was just perfect.

After some time, an extraterrestrial comes, and we peacefully communicate with him. Then, I give birth to a boy, and we return to humans. As it seems to me, it was either Bulgaria or the Czech Republic. There is a small town; we live there, and I'm a healer who assists in childbirth, engages in treatment, and communicates with people. At some point, there is a war; the town is attacked, but we aren't conquered, and there are minimal casualties. My husband makes weapons and ornaments from metal. Then I age, and the gift of foresight opens up to me; I can tell people what awaits them. Then, together with my husband, I die. A unicorn comes for me, and along a glowing path, I move toward something bright. I return to a new life, like a new transformation. I am a very cruel person—a man—and most likely, I am a murderer. I am somewhere in Iraq or Iran, all in black clothes, like a ninja. I feel the need to kill, but I don't want to do it, so I join the army, where it is justified. I live this life, die, and am buried with honors as a valiant warrior. Then I am born again in Europe, around the 1800s. I engage in research; I study physical phenomena. Then, I realize that, because of my research, someone will invent the nuclear bomb in the future, and it terrifies me.

Therapist: A very vivid and colorful experience of reliving past incarnations. You can be regarded as a magnificent subject for studying the structure of our phylogenetic experience.

Isabella: For me, any meditation always takes me somewhere I don't understand. Here, there are no images at all. I can't concentrate because my collarbone and neck hurt very badly, as if I'm being chopped with a sword. Everything burns, and it hurts so much that I can't bear it anymore. Well, when they said it was all over, that's when it all started for me. The image was like this: all chromosomes move inside a cell, and everything starts unfolding from there. I didn't remember; it was unimportant to me. The images were very beautiful, black-neon. But this pain in my body just irritates me and frustrates me.

Therapist: Perhaps you could go through several breathing sessions until all the accumulated emotional and muscular blocks find their release. Although the process may take some time, it's all very individual. During the sessions, just focus on your breath and allow the unconscious to regulate the process of emotional release. Sooner or later, the cleansing will happen.

Sophia: My body began to live a life of its own, separate from me. It was twisting me. When I was twisted very strongly, it felt like a crowd of people was around me. A very tight circle. I kept yawning, and it was difficult to control my breathing.

Peter: There was no effect for a long time. But then there was a feeling of some detachment from the body. It was a completely new sensation, and it was followed by my first vision during a holotropic breathing session. I looked inside a predatory creature. It was walking through some European cities, searching for something near buses and bus stops. It searched for a long time, and its gaze didn't stop at anything. There were some vague visions too, but I won't remember them.

James: Due to the pain in my chest during breathing, I had images from a book I had recently read and finished two weeks ago. It was a book about a concentration camp, and that's why I was constantly there. The piercing pain in my chest and numbness didn't allow me to breathe completely. I can say that I re-experienced the feelings reflected in the book.

Therapist: Yes, indeed, if you have recently watched a movie or read literature, the plot of these works can become part of the holotropic experience. But it's not all superficial. What we read and watch affects the content of our consciousness, so even if the plot is clearly influenced by something external, it is still a part of us and has significance.

Luna: I had a vision that I was a dancer in some tribe, all in feathers, very beautiful. I danced in front of the elders in a circle near a bonfire. Then, I was sold something similar, like an exotic creature, and I sailed on a canoe. After that, I found myself in a harem where I was very different from the others, with my luxurious hair, and the other girls felt strong envy toward me. Then, there were some vague images, and after that, I clearly saw my real life: my childhood and memories related to my brother. I relived that bright and strong feeling of love from childhood. Then, my brother and I dealt with an apartment that wasn't being rented out, and we managed to reach an agreement. The image was that I was in Germany with my brother, and we found common ground. Inside, there was a sense of joy and satisfaction.

Evelyn: The first state was stiffness in the shoulder girdle, as if I were being held by the shoulders and my back was arched at the knees. Next, there was a very strong heaviness in my arms, as if I were in chains—some kind of shackles. There was a strong sense of helplessness, as if I were bound to a rock and couldn't escape from there. I remember that I could fly, but now I'm told that I can never do that. Afterward, I realized that my hands were deformed—more specifically, they were broken. Then, somehow, I left there and met a man in the guise of a wise teacher. He told me that in life, complex situations happen that one must go through to learn and further develop. By the sensations, this happened in India. I am with this person, and I start learning: how to heal people, psychology, medicine, communication with nature, etc. Various people come to me in need of different kinds of assistance, and I provide that help. There is a slight chaos around me, but I continue to learn. I believe that everything will be fine. Then, my hand starts bothering me again, even though it has healed, but a certain injury still lingers. I communicate a lot with nature. There was a sensation of touching a tree or a lotus flower. I also saw spiders, but I reacted to them normally. I feel nature and all its diversity: plants, animals, people, and so on. Furthermore, at some point, I know that someone has come and desires my death. I don't want to die, but a noose appears in front of me, which is placed around my neck. At that moment, I transform and turn into a dove or some white butterfly that leaves everything behind and flies away to a completely different place. In the new place, I continue to learn, develop, and help people. I also remember that I acquired the ability to transform into different animals.

Charlotte: I had two lives. In the first one, I was a Native American playing musical instruments in harmony with nature. After that, something happened, and I died and ended up in hell. I went through all the circles of hell, and there was fire again. After that, there was silence. But, at some point, there was a click, and I saw the future. I was in a white dress, walking down the aisle. Another click, and I observed that, on one side, there were children, and on the other, my beloved work.

Mia: There was darkness that accompanied the entire holotropic session. During this session, I worked through four symptoms that bothered me. There were images, but they often changed and disappeared.

Emma: From the beginning, the images and sounds were frightening. There was an image of death, like a woman in a black veil and a black cloak. She approached and wanted to cover me. There were rivers of blood and mountains of human bodies. Human bodies were piled on top of each other, up to the very top. Then, an image of the devil followed, but it was somewhat unnatural, with disproportionate horns and hooves. It was terrifying. I constantly had the thought that I needed to run because death was chasing me, and I was in a panic. I heard bullets whizzing behind me, and I immediately associated it with my great-grandmother, who used to talk about how she had managed to avoid death several times. I started experiencing severe headaches and nausea and began to tremble. I wanted to run, and I was already contemplating where I could go to hide from death.

Day Two: Feedback After the Breathwork Session

Therapist: How are you all feeling? I'd like to know if you've had any special experiences between yesterday and today. Were there any significant dreams or unique states of mind?

Evelyn: I'm in good spirits, eager to experience something new.

Mia: I'm concerned about refining the emotional states I experienced yesterday, and that's my primary focus now.

Luna: I expect to derive pleasure and resolve some of my deep-seated issues.

Charlotte: My mood is good, and my expectations are positive. We'll see how it goes.

Sophia: I had an anxious dream, and I woke up several times during the night. Some fortune teller appeared in my dream and told me something. Also, the tension in my neck and shoulders has eased.

Therapist: When we observe muscle tension in the trapezius and neck muscles, it signifies fixation on one's personality and routine. I've mentioned this during our seminar. I'd like to add that spasms and tension in this area are expressions of unresolved personal conflicts. Behind the tension lies an emotion that seeks an outlet for expression, but for some reason, our superego, our moral conscience, prohibits this emotion from surfacing. The stronger the tension, the more profound the inner prohibition. Often, it takes a considerable amount of time to get to the essence of these restrictions and work through them to some extent. The neurosis of the superego can be quite despotic. Through the prism of our superego, we engage in a specific form of self-punishment for any moral transgressions we have committed in the past. Until we convince ourselves that we are capable of conforming to certain rules, our superego may make our mental and physical lives less enjoyable. Therefore, in the context of somatic and respiratory practices, it is, in my opinion, crucial to work with traditional verbal therapy, which can place emphasis where the flow of potent emotional energies, released during Holotropic breathwork, cannot achieve the necessary delicate therapeutic effect. It's essential to understand and consider this. Sometimes, therapy requires explosive, profound changes in a patient's consciousness to facilitate a shift in the right direction. Other times, it demands very subtle and detailed work on the awareness of small, sometimes microscopic cognitive and emotional processes within the individual to optimize their overall functionality. By the way, this is why ordinary massage procedures and similar spa treatments very rarely yield a complete therapeutic effect. No matter how much someone kneads a person's muscular blocks, without comprehensive therapy, things often revert to the same old patterns after some time. Unfortunately, that's a fact.

Peter: Nothing particularly unusual. The whole evening was quite relaxed, and sleep was somewhat restless, filled with a series of dark and gloomy dreams with an unpleasant atmosphere.

Therapist: Tell me, please, do you have them often?

Peter: No, there was just an oppressive atmosphere present in all the dreams, although the subjects were different.

Therapist: After holotropic breathing, we can stay for some time in those layers of experience that we touched during the breathing technique. Various forms of emotional pre-response may occur. This is absolutely normal. As a consequence, during some nights in dreams or states we experience in ordinary life, we can observe a strange emotional background.

Holotropic breathing sometimes gives only an opportunity to touch feelings but not to react fully. Only the subsequent breathing helps to enter this state again and allows this feeling to come out completely. I've had examples of people breathing for many sessions in a row and saying that it was as if they were touching something sad. Tears started to flow, and they didn't know why this was happening. It is only after a certain number of breathing sessions that a person can fully immerse themselves in the traumatic state and have a powerful reaction and release of feelings.

I see such clamps, for example, in girls and women who have had the experience of sexual seduction. There is a feeling in holotropic breathing as if there were some interactions in early childhood with some person. There is a feeling of disgust and anger, but no understanding of what is happening. The girl begins to breathe holotropically; after the session, she does not come out of the trance state. She begins to behave in highly unusual ways, crawls on the floor, and expresses a demonic face.

Once, such a patient crawled from the breathing room to the toilet. She crawled. I went after her; she crawled up to me and, in the hallway, grabbed my leg and looked at me with wild eyes that spoke of inhumanity. After a while, she started breathing again and went into a holotropic trance.

She tried to access the traumatic experience for more than four sessions in a row, and it was not until the fourth session that she had a spontaneous entry into certain memories from when she was 9 or 10 years old. She remembered her parents putting her in dance classes. She recalled that the teacher there was an extremely obnoxious man who smiled disgustedly and sweetly when he saw her. But she couldn't remember what happened there—a complete memory blockage. A feeling emerged that there was something there that was better not remembered. This was followed by a catharsis, a violent display of emotion, or an abreaction. It is only after a while that the discomfort that was in her body comes out completely. And then she is no longer immersed in a traumatic re-experience but in a transpersonal pleasant journey.

Often, holotropic breathing helps enter the state of trauma and react to it without providing a full understanding of what is going on, but the feelings come out of the person.

Sometimes a person gets the opportunity for a journey that is more distant and more interesting, which is less saturated with routine experiences and has a relationship to archetypal processes that are connected to the memory of our ancestors. Associating oneself with shamans, with animals, and with natural phenomena—this indicates that either the person has managed to react to some meaningful feeling or his defense mechanisms easily let him into this space for some other reason. If you are quick to enter the transpersonal experience, it doesn't mean that you don't have unreacted emotions and feelings; maybe you just skip past them too quickly.

Amelia: I'm doing well; something was dreamt of, but I can't remember what. I think it was something pleasant, as there are no discomforting states. I usually wake up tired and irritated, but today everything feels light and comfortable. I'm very content, and I've gained a sense of wholeness and integrity. I live and do what's needed in the moment. Peacefulness. Also, I had back pain, but now the pain is gone.

Isabella: My shoulders still hurt a lot, and I'm very frightened after yesterday. Everything is frightening. The dreams were very interesting. I always have very interesting dreams, and you could write novels based on them. But today, neon-colored tiger cubs were chasing me, and then I turned into the wind... Well, I had many dream plots, and I didn't even try to remember them. But overall, there's a state of anxiety and this pain that I don't know what to do about. It hurts all the time, both now and at night.

Ava: Well, I don't know if it's because of the holotropic experience or after dental treatment. I decided that I needed to learn to knit with needles and a hook. I already have yarn and a hook here. Today, I went to the store to see my friend and decided that I really needed this.

Therapist: Many people who come for holotropic breathing for the first time experience phobic reactions about what they're about to do. Fear is a classic reaction. When I ask them what holotropic feels like to them, they often say it's as if they're going to take drugs or that something bad might happen to them. The more feelings that are unreacted to in our consciousness and in our body, the more phobic reactions can arise regarding the practice of the technique. I've repeatedly observed such negative projections using hypnotic techniques. What we don't understand well potentially triggers anxious states. The stronger the various suppressed emotions, the stronger the anxiety may be before the practice itself.

Somatic Approach in Breathwork Therapy

Now, I would like to show you a bit of the bodywork element so that you understand what I can do with you and your body during Holotropic breathwork sessions if there is any therapeutic necessity. Yesterday, I didn't need to work with you using somatic practices, as you managed the work yourself quite well. Here's a brief explanation.

During the Holotropic breathwork seminar, I provide instructions on how it should proceed, and if you are working as a facilitator, I guide you on how to interact with your patient. One of the natural reactions that may occur in a patient during a breathing session is motor activity. A typical element is hand-drumming on the floor. If I observe that a patient is making such movements and if I see that they are excessive and overly intense, I can approach the patient, take hold of their hands from both sides, and ask them to continue the emerging reactive movement. This way, we can effectively block hand movements and accelerate abreactive motor processes in the patient's behavior. By observing the intensity of a patient's motor reactions, you can adjust the force and intensity of the blockage. It's worth explaining here that sometimes a simple motor representation of emotions is already a full abreaction. However, at times, excessive and strong movements that persist for quite a while indicate that, for some reason, the emotion cannot fully express itself and needs external resistance, which can be used as a kind of starting point to initiate a complete abreaction. Compression and blockage effectively transition the patient to the third perinatal matrix. The phase of struggle, which sooner or later must end with resolution, can sometimes trigger the transition from the second perinatal matrix to the third. This can provide the patient with significant improvement and move them forward. However, it is necessary to have some experience working with patients in the context of Holotropic breathwork to understand when such somatic interventions are appropriate and when they can be omitted.

We can observe various leg movements. A patient lying on the mat may start waving their legs, tapping, lifting and lowering them, twisting, and so on. If you try to work with a patient whose legs are swinging vigorously, remember that legs are very strong parts of the body, and you may get injured if you inadvertently get in the way. Innocent leg waving on the surface can hide a very high energetic potential, so be cautious. Working with the legs can be done as follows: you lie in the area of the patient's knees and stabilize their body. While energy is being released, you hold the legs, but when it subsides, you release the patient and conclude work with that part of the body.

Another point of attention fixation is the arching of the body—fixation on the shoulders and arching like a bridge. Some individuals may do this spontaneously and with weak intensity, while others arch their bodies like this and remain in that position for many minutes in a row. In my practice, there have been moments when I was held in this position for up to 10 minutes. Some patients perform these movements in a jerky manner, arching and lowering themselves sharply several times in a row. If you see this form of work, you position yourself around the patient in a specific way and instruct them to continue arching. For a while, you will be pushed upward, and you need to use your body weight to create additional resistance to the emotional energy that is being released during the breathing process. In the vast majority of cases, this form of somatic work does not require much. Only a few patients arch their backs like a bridge. However, if this happens, it indicates very strong emotions, often breaking through from the transpersonal sphere beyond the individual self. Usually, after several arches of the back, patients feel relief, and the intensity of their emotions decreases.

Some patients start moving their heads vigorously in different directions, as if they have head tremors. In such cases, you approach the person from behind the head in a specific manner and use your hands to hold their head from both sides. You should apply pressure, but very gently, to avoid injuring the neck, focusing the pressure on the sides of the temples. Remember that during this movement, there may be other body movements. Focus on one thing and then move on to another and a third, as needed.

Another crucial point of attention is that some people may dive into states of perinatal matrices and actively re-experience them. How can you tell if a person has entered the first perinatal matrix?

The patient begins to draw their knees toward themselves, turning to the side. When you see that a person assumes this position, you should approach them and continue working with them. What do you do? You approach them and become, metaphorically, a mother figure. You embrace them and provide a sense of contact.

After some time, you can begin to create artificial spasms by compressing the patient's body from all sides as much as possible. During this, the patient may regress even deeper into the process of rebirth and start providing feedback in the form of moans and other auditory and somatic signals. After a while, you can release the full-body grip and, holding the patient's hands, start pulling them forward, thus simulating the process of leaving the womb.

After some time, you will notice that the legs straighten, indicating that your patient has been born, emerging from the womb. When they have emerged from the womb, you need to provide them with a sense of contact again. You can embrace them briefly and spend some time with them.

Stay with them for a while, embracing them and simulating maternal movements and contact. Then leave them, but continue to observe what happens next. This is elementary bodywork during the process of holotropic breathing, and it's something worth paying attention to. During this rebirthing work, a therapist and one or two assistants may be involved. However, in real practice, we often don't have such luxury and must make do with the available resources. One therapist should be capable of carrying out the entire procedure alone.

Feedback: Third Breathwork Session

Mia: I drew a clock mechanism. I didn't have any images for a long time. Then, at some point, I returned to childhood. There were a few more images, but I can't recall them clearly. The last image that came was one of being rocked in a cradle.

Evelyn: I felt like a snake crawling among the grass. Then I transformed into a bird—some prehistoric lizard, a pterodactyl. I transformed several times into different animals. Then I became a native somewhere in Africa. I remember being among animals and learning to interact with them and feel them. I touched the foreheads of tigers, crocodiles, and so on. I felt no fear, even though I knew they were all predators. My fear came when I encountered birds like crows, etc. Anything related to danger from above was very frightening for me. It felt safer below, and for a while, I was a native. Then came a period of darkness. After that, images reappeared as if I were a spider but an animal. In this form, I have teeth, and I eat. My state was melancholic. I spent my time sleeping and eating fruits. Then I seemed to fall again and remember nothing. The next thing I remember is entering a tunnel, but it's not scary because it's short, and I know something awaits beyond it. Then, I simply walk down a road, striving for something and needing to reach somewhere. Eventually, I arrive at the sea, where I see the sun.

I approach the sea, transform into a fish, and then back into a human who sails on a ship, following the sun to a new land like an explorer. I had a sense of anticipation for something new and exciting.

Charlotte: Initially, I had an image of myself, from which another being emerged, also a girl but much larger. Initially, everything was fine: music, flowers, nature, and travel. Then, an image of a road appeared with a car driving on it and nothing else. In the end, I saw a red tree on which pears were growing. I plucked these pears, although I didn't eat them, and I don't even know why I did it.

Luna: I expected lightness but experienced something emotionally complex and heavy. My breathing was interrupted, and I felt pain in the solar plexus area. Unfortunately, I didn't see any images. I was just waiting for it to end. For me, this was a very unpleasant and heavy session.

Ava: It's when I started crawling on the mat and beyond it. The most vivid part was when I re-experienced "Alice in Wonderland." I had a very long neck at times or very long legs that didn't fit, and the mat was so small. It was all very tangled but very vivid. There was a fantastic tea party with the Mad Hatter. I liked that when falling into the rabbit hole, I experienced it as a descent, not a fall. Afterward, I felt like the leader of wolves in Odin's retinue, and there were ravens. Then I saw a fiery rooster with tongues of flame instead of feathers. Next, I was an Egyptian priestess in a temple of a goddess associated with cats. The following image was of me in spring, as the snow melted, grass sprouted, and flowers bloomed. Then I was in a post-apocalyptic world. I was a barbarian woman on a bear wearing metallic armor. Then I saw people with bird heads. After that, I flew on a griffin, and others were also flying on griffins and pegasi nearby. There were also sea turtles flying through the air.

Isabella: An image came to me that I felt. It was a girl, a very beautiful girl. She was a gymnast or a ballerina, and she was inside me. I saw this as a street lamp, and she was suspended from it by her leg. It seemed like it was me. Another peculiarity of today's session is that I was descending somewhere. I forgot to breathe and was descending, but where I was going, I don't know. My shoulders and neck continued to bother me a lot, although there were moments when I found a comfortable position, and it was easier for me. But my body was restless; it would ache, burn, or throb.

Olivia: Immediately, I had the image that I was a sperm, but I was contemplating. After all, it should carry a lot of useful and good information. Various images followed: me on a horse by the sea, traveling, and so on. Then, I became a mountaineer, climbing mountains, and at some point, I fell into an abyss, falling backward, crashing into rocks, and dying. There was no pain, just realization, but it was very difficult for my soul to leave my body; I couldn't accept that it was over. I wanted to tear open my chest so it could depart. Finally, I managed to ascend, appearing like a white dove. Below, I saw my broken body in blood—a man in a red suit, mountaineering gear. I ascended very high, knowing there was a special station there, and I had to reach it. Flying was very challenging; my wings grew tired, and my heart raced. Finally, with one last effort, I grasped onto a threshold, as if I had swum to the pool's edge. I entered, and on an altar, I saw a book. I opened it to the page I needed; it described a person, my new incarnation on Earth, with all the information about their tasks, abilities, and obstacles. There was some darkness or uncertainty around the ages of 13–14, which troubled me. I closed the book, walked out, and descended to Earth as a ray. There, I found my future parents and merged with them to later become whole. Then, I was a sperm again, now with all this knowledge, meeting an egg. This time, everything developed continuously, and everything was good. I was born, grew up, and before my eyes, there were events from my life. When adolescence arrived, I realized that I had been watching how my parents were not doing very well, and I was always "daddy's little girl," and he was the most handsome man for me. I wished my chosen one would be like him. My mom didn't support my dad, and it saddened me. I believed I could have taken better care of him. I feel like I betrayed him twice: when I loved him more than with daughterly love, and when I ran away from all the family problems, trying to build my own life with an older man. If I had acted more wisely and consciously, maybe I would still have my father. I see his grave; I sit in front of it, crying and asking for forgiveness for all this. I couldn't leave for a long time, but eventually, I left the cemetery calm; I had let him go. Next, the image: I'm an 18-year-old girl in a white dress, happy, leaping down the steps—I've successfully passed all the exams—a scene like in a familiar movie, one to one.

Emma: There were many different images. I don't know why I drew this because there were only snakes, eyes, and a tortoise. From the very beginning, the pictures frequently changed. I remember there were many snakes coiling around hands and fingers. A tortoise was walking on the sand. Then there was some witch in black clothing, and I heard church bells ringing. Afterward, there were women's eyes—eyes of various women. There was an image of a full white moon. I relived the lives of each woman whose eyes I saw. These women were all of easy virtue with difficult fates. Right now, I want to tear my drawing to pieces. I won't, but I really want to.

Peter: There was no actual vision, but there were feelings that I was spinning and being pulled somewhere. It felt like being inside some kind of tube, which stopped being a tube entirely, leading to complete emptiness and comfort. I wanted to curl up or hold onto something. I enjoyed this state.

Sophia: My drawing has no relation to my experience. I was drawing whatever came to mind without thinking. There were many emotions. At the beginning, I felt very small and sensed a close spiritual connection with my dad, which brought me a painful feeling that caused me to start crying. Then I felt like a woman giving birth to a child, experiencing contractions, and my hands were sweating heavily. The drawing shows that life emerges from nothing.

Amelia: It started with me living in a camp, not a wealthy one, and I was a ten-year-old girl. Then I saw a rabbit running away. I chased the rabbit, with a wolf following immediately behind us, from which we were running away. There was no danger; it felt like a game. Then we went somewhere with the wolf and the rabbit. First, we were in a forest, and then we ended up in India in some city with many people. I couldn't find my place and sat down, looking at a pond with fish swimming in it. Then I turned into a fish and swam into the sea. I swam across the sea, then approached an island and transformed into some sort of lizard. After that, I turned into a monkey, and then I transformed into a human. There was an image of a wolf, and I was seeing the world through its eyes. Then I returned again, and I was a girl working in a circus with poisonous snakes, crocodiles, pumas, and lynxes. I admired the acrobats and wanted to try their skills. I climbed onto the trapeze, fell from it, and shattered. The next image was of me lying in a grave, seeing a monument above me, and I felt very sad that I had broken. Then, I realized my spirit was returning and experiencing a new life. At that moment, I understood that I would have broken anyway, even if I had been an acrobat since childhood. New images appeared in which I saw a castle. I became a conqueror, like a Viking. I conquered the castle and killed everyone. I became a very harsh ruler of this castle, feared by all. Then, not to reveal my weakness and not to die of old age, I had to jump off a cliff. I stood on the edge; there was fog, and I couldn't jump. I was very scared. But eventually, I fell and shattered. I lay at the bottom, and at that moment, spiders came to me and started eating me. It was frightening and disgusting. Then I realized that I had to run, and that was the only way I could save myself. I ran very fast, and the faster I ran, the quicker I hid from death. She was right behind me, and I realized that no matter how much I ran, she would catch up to me eventually. I turned around, and something amorphous met me—a black void. It was very scary, and later, I saw it as a skeleton. After that, I dissolved and left. My spirit flew away. Only through flight could I save myself. The house in the drawing is where I'll be safe.

Sophia: I felt myself in the body of my fictional character. Everything around me was in ruins, as if a war or some battle had taken place. I began to realize that, at that moment, I had lost everything I had. Everyone close to me, everything, completely everything. I was left alone, and I would remain alone. I felt so lonely; this feeling emotionally tore me apart. I knew I wasn't to blame for anything, but I still blamed myself for not being able to help. Tears flowed on their own, like waterfalls. At some point, I stood up and started walking along the road. I didn't care at all about what would happen to me next. I couldn't see any more meaning in my existence. I walked utterly empty, devoid of any emotions. The cold, skin-piercing wind blew into my face, and cars rushed by. I didn't care that I could die at that moment. They could hit me; well, so be it. That's how I walked and slowly began to disintegrate into black smoke. First my legs, then upwards through my body. Then, suddenly, I saw the sun rising on the horizon, how there was life on that same horizon, and that there was no destruction there, which had been behind me. I continued walking toward that life. A person approached me and said that losing everything doesn't mean it's the end. There will be something new ahead. And I believed him. I had no other way out. I followed him. Then I remember sitting in nature, perhaps meditating or just sitting. But I felt how nature filled me with its strength and gave me energy. A gentle breeze blew and seemed to permeate me. I felt like I was that breeze. And then I felt a tremendous surge of power. I held the power of nature in my hands. I could control its elements. Somehow, it was air and fire. I stood up and walked down the road. There seemed to be fog. I saw the one who deprived me of everything I had. I wanted to take revenge. By the way, this someone was coming to take my life too, but I wasn't afraid of them. I knew for sure that today was not their day and that they would die. And it happened. I felt so much energy under my command, as if now all the laws of nature were subordinate to me, as if I were nature itself. I leveled that person with the earth. And after that, I couldn't calm down; the power was just bursting out of me. I clearly remember having black eyes, like demons in movies. I continued walking. I didn't need to wave my hands to control the energy; I just walked, and a hurricane rose around me, sweeping everything away with just one thought. It seemed to me that this world had become so impure that it was time to destroy it and cleanse it, even if it had to be done with blood. I continued walking, purifying this world and this planet. After the wind, everything started to ignite. Not just catching fire like a candle, but erupting into a blazing wall of flames. I remember that at the very end of my apocalypse, two enormous fireballs swept by and burned down everything that remained. Chaos ensued again, after which everything began to be reborn. I looked at the new people and the new world and thought that I had indeed cleansed the world, that now everything would be different, and if necessary, I would destroy it all over again, that the Earth had been reborn.

Feedback: Fourth Breathwork Session

Olivia: Central street of my city, sunny weather, summer; then I see people flying like in "The Matrix." Then I see a lake, and someone in it wants to drown me. I resist, but I drown, and I die. Then spiders crawl out of my mouth; it's disgusting, and I'm afraid of them. And then I turn into a spider myself, and I'm scared of them—big people are walking nearby; they could crush me. I want to hide in a corner somewhere. Then I think about where spiders can live safely, and I teleport to the tropics. There, I am a lovely orange and black furry spider, living safely. Then I visit other spiders in other safe places—a desert, jungles, and so on. Then I travel on a ship from distant lands, perched on the captain's shoulder as a spider, sailing somewhere.

My real self begins to ponder: Why am I doing all this? Probably, I can take something useful or good from them—agility or swiftness. A human spider, of course, is good, but not entirely beautiful, in my opinion. I think about which other animals I could temporarily unite with to acquire useful qualities. Oh, a cat—that's super—flexibility, agility, grace, the ability to relax and instantly focus—we take it. A dog—friendliness, the ability to enjoy life, loyalty—we take it. A horse—strength, endurance, beauty, confidence—we take it. With all these animals, I somehow energetically unite, take their abilities, fill myself with them, and then let go.

Then I realize that I possess extraordinary abilities; I can heal. I understand that I am a witch, but not an evil one; I help people. But not everyone likes those who stand out. A crowd that doesn't understand something can destroy you. And for some reason, men can pose the greatest danger to me. I have observed myself being killed several times, as a witch, very cruelly—stoned, hanged, impaled, tied to horses by hands and feet, drowned—and men do this. I hear the sound of a drum; at first, it attracts me—it gives me strength. But upon realizing that a man is playing it, I try to move away as far as possible on a carpet.

I, an adult witch, tell my daughter, a future witch: "You can't trust men; they are dangerous and cruel to women because they don't understand us. They are afraid that we know too much and can do too much, so they destroy us. It's safe while you're still a child, and they don't know who you are or when you're unattractive; that deters them somewhat. Or you can be beautiful but stupid, but being both beautiful and smart is very dangerous. Either learn to hide well or become very strong, but it's best if you're one of them—a man. Only a man can live to a ripe old age and die as a respected, wise man."

I want to live, and I don't want to hide, so I gather others like me. We are in the forest on a clearing, saddling horses with bows on our shoulders and swords on our belts. I am ready to fight with men, those who can harm me, and to defend myself.

Emma: Again, there were many images of promiscuous girls. Then there were discomforting sensations in my body. The music playing triggered an emotional upheaval in me. I wanted to show the world my colorful mood and release all my aggression. After painting all of this, I felt relieved. Right now,

I feel magnificent.

Ava: For me, this session was quite dramatic. I decided to focus on my father. Among the images, there was the sky, a planet, a white fluffy ball—that's me—and a black hole that sucked in my dad. It was very unpleasant when my body moved on its own. Then I felt better, and an image of a pregnant woman protecting her child with her hand appeared. Everything became colorful and peaceful.

Isabella: I have nothing to share. From session to session, the pain keeps increasing. I want to eliminate this pain, but I can't. In the end, I saw images. It was like an atomic explosion in reverse. Various colors emerged. I asked a question about how the events happening in our country would end, and there was a gray-black picture with a crystallizing snowflake.

Peter: Nothing special happened. My jaw clenched horribly again, and most of my body was affected. At first, I struggled with it for a long time. Then I relaxed and entered a semi-dream state.

Sophia: At first, there was an image like in "The Lord of the Rings"—a cave with spider webs and a big spider. I couldn't hide anywhere; I knew I had nowhere to escape. I was restless, trying to find a place, but I couldn't. There was only one way out—a cliff. Either I jump from the height or the spider eats me. I was afraid of both spiders and heights. Then a transformation occurred, where I became a spirit and flew away. I flew like a butterfly or a fairy—beautiful and with wings. I felt no fear, and I wouldn't die. I saw people and their suffering, which didn't affect me. But I still transformed into these people and experienced several lives where I was tortured, crucified, and died painfully. Then I found myself back in the same cave, and I was just scared. I thought that, lying down, spiders might crawl into my mouth, so I got on all fours. Then childhood memories emerged. I saw the house where I lived with my father. I saw many scary and sad pictures. I screamed and wanted to stop what was happening there, but I couldn't stop it. Then I was at the cemetery. I realized I didn't want to live. Next, I continued to sit there; my brother appeared, and we sat together. It happened as it should have. Outside the gates, we met our mom. We were all together, but each had their own life, and we went our separate ways. There were images from childhood where I was a little girl walking with my dad. Then an image appeared where I was in a light, transparent cloak, and it was my protection from everything, thanks to my father. If I have children, it will be a memory and a source of gratitude. I wanted to paint a family where I am with my husband and three children. Here, I am in the image of a swan princess.

Sophia: (very expressive feedback) It all began with me finding myself in the corridor of some office building where the lights were turned off. For some reason, I had a Japanese sword in my hands. Then I was transported to another place. In front of me appeared a naked woman with earthy bluish, scaly skin, completely black eyes (those eyes again), and hair slicked back. In her hands, I was like a puppet; she could do whatever she wanted with me, and I didn't resist much. She transported me and herself to a Gothic-style castle resembling a Catholic church. She threw me against a column, and I sat on the floor. Then she started dancing some kind of dance. She moved in a circle, igniting torches or candles around the hall in the castle. As she danced, she would either break into something resembling shards of black glass or spread across the floor like some dark liquid. I remember she even made me cut my own hand with the sword. Then an angel appeared, in a long white robe with white wings and hair. He reached out his hand to help me stand— a helping hand, so to speak. We stood like that for a long time, and I believed in the angel, believing that he would save me. After a while, the angel's eyes turned black, then his skin became scaly, but I continued to believe, as if not noticing that it was not an angel but the same woman transformed into him. The woman started dancing again, causing the building's walls to crumble. Then she stood behind me. The sun rose on the horizon. Our castle was on some hill, and from there, I could see the city where people lived their lives below. The woman whispered in my ear that all those people were running like squirrels on a wheel, that they had neither strength nor choice. And she had given me the strength to fight. Her words were something like that. And I actually felt some power in myself—not supernatural, just an energy surge. I was no longer a puppet in the woman's hands. I turned around and saw a man not far from me, muscular, with the same earthy color and hair resembling worms. That's how his hair looked. In general, I had to fight him. He was stronger than me—much stronger—but I believed in my own strength. Even after he created the illusion of a round room with walls and a floor made of stone, he was in control. He pushed my face into the wall. Then a lake filled with liquid metal appeared between us. I understood that he was afraid of fire. I don't remember why I thought that, but I took a torch from the wall and threw it into the lake. A small wall of fire rose, and the man recoiled. Then I took a match and threw it into the lake as well. The man caught fire and fell. His illusions began to crumble, and I found myself again in the ruined room of the Gothic castle. Now I had to confront the woman, which I did. After that, the sun rose on the horizon, and instead of high-rise city buildings, there were trees and streams. A man approached me and told me that I had achieved cosmic self-awareness in the game of self-discovery, Lila. I had conquered my fears (embodied by the man) and thus won. I truly felt different—stronger, calmer, more confident, and wiser. We walked along the road. The man told me that now all doors were open to me—absolutely all. Doors appeared against the backdrop of nature. I chose one and entered it. I found myself in a dark room where I stood before myself, but without a face. The other me somehow made me fall, as if she wanted to drink my soul. I aged and grew young again during her actions. In the end, my face ended up on hers. The room disappeared, and the other "me" began to fade away. I realized that I had landed not on cell 68 of cosmic awareness (the game ends there), but on cell 72, where I was bitten by the snake Tamas and returned to the Earth cell, from which I had to go back to cell 68 (referring to the board game "Lila Chakra"). If I find my way and take back my face from Tamas, then the game will end. I stood up and started walking along the road. I remember that I walked for a long time, and beneath my path, I saw some cities where people were crying out. Looking at them, for some reason, I decided that not having a face was not the biggest problem in life and that those people had it worse. In the end, I finally found Tamas. As I approached her, it became increasingly difficult to move, but I still reached her. She returned my face to me, after which I found myself in a beautiful place.

I thought I was in heaven. I felt completely different. I had really become wiser and had achieved a connection with the cosmos. I remember communicating with my daughter. She was to return to Earth to be born with her soul but with my body, and I would get a new body. We would meet when she, like me, had reached cosmic knowledge. When my daughter went to Earth, the celebration began. I and other people who had reached cosmic cognition started dancing and having fun. Then I returned to Earth. The people who were at my level of self-knowledge saw me, but the others did not. I was walking for a long time, and then I began to realize that I was forgetting everything that was happening to me. I was surrounded by some kind of cocoon from which I had to crawl out and be reborn. I crawled out and started to peel off my skin like clothes to get to my real body. For a long time, I peeled off my skin layer by layer and finally found myself in my new body. I was born again in a new life.

Luna: I had body work. My posture changed because my legs were numb. At the moment when I changed my posture, streams of images began to flow—they were memories of all the sexual violence that had happened to me. I saw them as slides that changed from one to another. I began to wonder why I was doing this, but there was no emotion, and the answer was "to not be afraid of men." There was some kind of parting, as it seemed to me (Luna had more than 20 cases of individual sexual violence and several cases of group sexual violence).

Isabella: There was a solution to everything, or so it seemed to me. I had two clients that I refused because I didn't know how to work with them. And in the Holotropic session, I saw that I was able to help them with art therapy. Then there was the rebirth process with me. Next, there were a lot of vivid childhood images. There is an image of my father, which leads me to a picture with gypsies, and I think there is some connection with Tarot cards.

Charlotte: At first, I had darkness. Next, I saw the glare of colored music. The next image was the wind, which was stirring the ears in the field, and I was standing alone in the middle of the field. I just stayed silent and touched the tall ears of wheat. Another image was that I was climbing trees like Tarzan.

Amelia: An image came as if I were riding a horse along the seashore. I am a woman. I have ridden the horse to the rocks, and I realize that I am waiting for my husband. It's not a war; I'm just waiting for his return and staring out to sea. Then, I get very worried and scratch my left arm, thinking that I may be in pain, but he will be alive. Next, I am transported to another place—I am skating on ice. There is darkness around me, and I am very scared because I can't see anything. But still, the day comes, and everything becomes calm. Then, I move to the forest, where I go skiing. Spring comes, and everything is blooming. I have blond hair, and I am practicing pottery. In the process of learning this skill, my injured hand heals. I make dishes out of clay, and my hands become soft and white because of it. I see that my hands are very beautiful. I do a lot of housework. I realize that I have children. Soon my husband will come back home. The next image is of me clearing and meditating. Then, I start circling in some kind of ritual dance and interacting with the energy. Through this energy, I can be transported into space. Next, I see my hands; on one of them is the Sun, and on the other is Saturn, and in the middle is the Moon. I feel like I am starting to juggle these celestial bodies. Then, there is an image of me as a six-year-old boy sitting on the shore of a lake and catching fish. It's not the food that matters to me but the childlike joy and harmony. I move back into my life. I am about three years old, and I feel lonely. I have a conversation with myself and reassure myself that I am always protected and can handle any difficulties.

Therapist: Throughout this seminar, you have gained a wealth of powerful and profound experiences, which, in my opinion, have the potential to significantly alter your life and your perception of the world. In addition to our work on emotions, I have endeavored to provide a brief yet comprehensive discussion of the fundamental aspects of working with the Holotropic Breathwork method. I hope that the experiences and information you have acquired will find a special and positive place in your consciousness, contributing to a more integrated and holistic life.

Physiological Aspects of Hyperventilation in Breathwork

In the human body, multiple metabolic processes occur simultaneously. To ensure these processes run smoothly, a continuous supply of oxygen and the removal of carbon dioxide are essential. This process in the human body is referred to as external respiration.

"Respiration is the sum of processes that provide the body with oxygen and remove carbon dioxide."

Respiration, therefore, constitutes one of the central functions governing the vital processes of the human body. The respiratory system (the respiratory tract) is responsible for this function in the human body. The respiratory system comprises the respiratory pathways, which, in turn, include nasal passages, the pharynx, the trachea, bronchi, and small bronchioles. The bronchi branch out and spread throughout the entire lung volume, resembling an inverted tree canopy. Oxygen, as part of the air, enters the lungs through the nasal passages, pharynx, and bronchi. The smallest bronchial endings terminate in numerous thin-walled pulmonary sacs known as alveoli.

Alveoli consist of 500 million tiny sacs, each with a diameter of 0.2 micrometers, where the exchange of oxygen into the bloodstream and the removal of carbon dioxide from the blood takes place. Gas exchange occurs within the alveoli, with oxygen transferring from the pulmonary sacs to the bloodstream while carbon dioxide moves from the bloodstream to the pulmonary sacs.

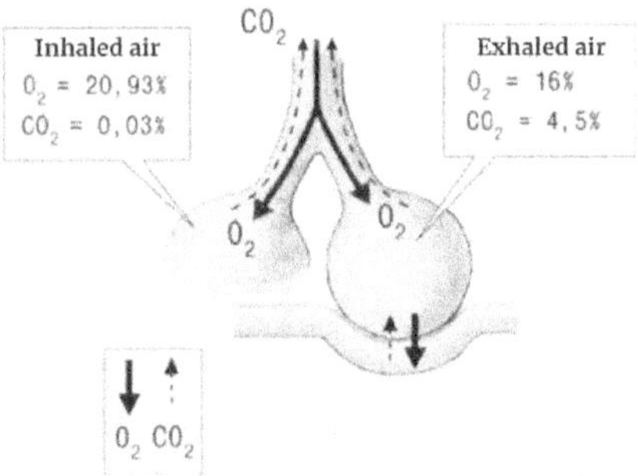

Pulmonary vesicle. Gas exchange in the lungs

One of the most crucial processes in gas exchange is diffusion, in which molecules move from an area of high concentration to an area of low concentration without the expenditure of energy—a phenomenon known as passive transport. Oxygen transfer from the surrounding environment to the cells occurs through the transport of oxygen into the alveoli and, subsequently, into the bloodstream. Consequently, venous blood becomes enriched with oxygen, transforming into arterial blood. Oxygen binds to hemoglobin, which is contained within erythrocytes. Blood saturated with oxygen is directed to the heart, pumped into the systemic circulation, and distributed to all organs and systems.

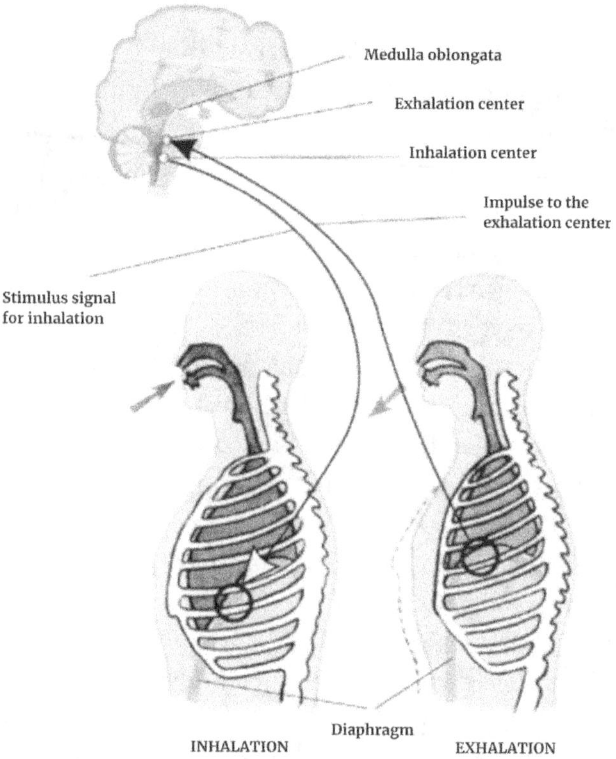
Medulla oblongata
Exhalation center
Inhalation center
Impulse to the exhalation center
Stimulus signal for inhalation
Diaphragm
INHALATION
EXHALATION

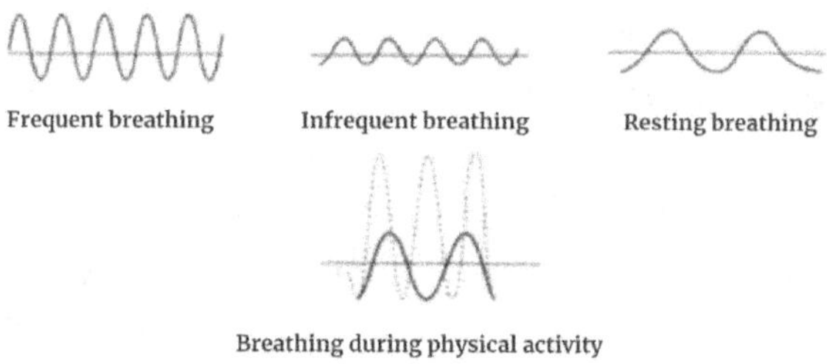
Frequent breathing
Infrequent breathing
Resting breathing
Breathing during physical activity

Hyperventilation in Breathwork

The term "hyperventilation," derived from Greek and Latin roots, translates to "intensive breathing," indicating an accumulation and increased demand for oxygen in the body by several times. Hyperventilation is characterized by deep and rapid breathing, during which ventilation and oxygen content, as well as the exhalation of carbon dioxide, significantly exceed the current norm required for the normal exchange of carbon dioxide and oxygen at that moment.

In the literature and textbooks on physiology, hyperventilation is described as a standard physiological response to increased breathing frequency. Symptoms include "carpopedal spasms" or tetany—involuntary jerking, muscle spasms in the hands and legs, and the release of neuromuscular locks. In some situations, individuals may experience chest pains, involuntary and unexplained increases in anxiety, which can escalate to panic attacks, and difficulties with inhalation and exhalation. In cases of prolonged uncontrolled hyperventilation, cerebral hypoxia may occur, leading to loss of consciousness. When symptoms of hyperventilation manifest, some authors recommend seeking immediate medical assistance. However, it is essential to note that not a single case of death from hyperventilation has been recorded or described. The assumption of a fatal outcome logically follows the escalation of symptoms, which is a misconception. The body's protective mechanisms inherently include the preservation of the organism.

There are several types of hyperventilation, including controlled and uncontrolled forms, as well as its manifestation as a symptom in certain medical conditions.

Breathing is a physiological process in which the entire

organism participates. Through respiration, the body carries out the act of breathing and gas exchange with the external environment. Under normal circumstances, the composition of gas exchange varies within limited conditions. During hyperventilation, at the onset of the breathing process, the initial oxygen level increases by 40–50% above the norm, while its concentration decreases significantly after a minute. Conversely, carbon dioxide (CO_2) levels markedly decrease during hyperventilation, and after a minute of breathing in this mode, the CO_2 content in the alveoli drops below normal, sometimes reaching prolonged levels during extended workouts. The state characterized by prolonged CO_2 reduction is termed hypocapnia.

Within the human body, a specific pH level in the environment is maintained. A shift towards alkalinity occurs in the lungs during hypocapnia, resulting from intense, deep, rhythmic breathing. This shift towards alkaline pH alters the activity of vitamins and enzymes, as well as the levels of oxygen and carbon dioxide. Metabolism regulators encompass enzymes, vitamins, oxygen, and carbon dioxide. During prolonged workouts, oxygen levels increase, but there is also a controlled increase in carbon dioxide.

The need for regular physical exertion more effectively alleviates the tension of hyperventilation and mitigates hypocapnia. To maintain the oxygen-carbon dioxide balance in the blood and the respiratory system of the human body, the following mechanisms exist:

Suspension and constriction of blood vessels and bronchi.

Increased production of biological insulator products, such as cholesterol, by the liver During periods of low oxygen levels and elevated carbon dioxide levels, cholesterol acts as a biological insulator, causing membrane thickening in blood vessels and the lungs.

An alteration of arterial blood pressure parameters, particularly a decrease, is known as hypotension. Under normal conditions, arterial blood pressure ranges from 110/70 to 120/80. However, hyperventilation leads to a decrease in alveolar pressure to levels as low as 100/60 and causes the restrained elimination of CO_2 from the body.

Vascular and Respiratory Impacts

Hyperventilation leads to the constriction of blood vessels and bronchi, thereby altering the oxygen supply to the cells of the brain, kidneys, liver, heart, and other organs and systems of the body. During hyperventilation, the inflow of CO_2 into the blood is significantly reduced, while the binding of oxygen to free hemoglobin in the blood increases. Paradoxically, this reduces the ability of oxygen to enter the cells. This phenomenon is known as the Bohr effect: a decrease in blood CO_2 content enhances the binding of oxygen to hemoglobin, simultaneously hindering oxygen entry into cells.

Alterations in blood oxygen content, specifically decreased blood oxygen levels and tissue oxygen influx over an extended period, result in tissue oxygen deprivation, a state known as hypoxia. Prolonged oxygen deprivation initially leads to a loss of consciousness, heightened focus on the act of breathing, bodily lightness and weakness, muscle relaxation, changes in skin coloration (pallor), and decreased attention, culminating in a loss of consciousness.

Hyperventilation is characterized by rapid, shallow breathing—tachypnea—without a decrease in tidal volume, resulting in increased minute ventilation and alveolar ventilation. Various types of hyperventilation are distinguished: transient hyperventilation and chronic hyperventilation (hyperventilation syndrome). At present, numerous factors can induce hyperventilation, particularly psychological and neurological disorders of the central and autonomic nervous systems in an adrenal type. Most often, nervous tension, exhaustion of the central nervous system, and the autonomic nervous system in an adrenal type become the causes of hyperventilation. The sympathoadrenal system, regulated by pituitary and hypothalamic hormones to maintain organism homeostasis, releases high doses of adrenaline into the blood. Elevated adrenaline levels lead to uncontrolled vasoconstriction and muscle contraction. This creates a vicious circle, with hyperventilation being one of its patterns. In this state, hyperventilation attacks can last for hours, with the typical duration of an attack being approximately 20–30 minutes. To restore carbon dioxide balance and prevent an attack, it is necessary to reestablish carbon dioxide levels in the blood. One of the ways to achieve this is by breathing into a paper bag or tightly cupped hands near the mouth, which allows the replenishment of exhaled carbon dioxide.

Controlled Hyperventilation

Controlled hyperventilation (voluntary) occurs when a person consciously breathes rapidly (practitioners of breath control techniques, rebirthing, holotropic breathing, the Wim Hof method, free breathing, shamans, and freedivers before immersion in water) or effectively utilizes the functioning of the bronchopulmonary system during physical exertion. This is a primary factor in activities such as diving, speleology, and various sports. To achieve an oxygen reserve before immersion or physical exertion, practitioners use hyperventilation, involving rapid inhalations and exhalations. During this process, all the physical effort is exerted during inhalation.

Uncontrolled Hyperventilation

Uncontrolled hyperventilation (involuntary) can occur as a result of intense physical exertion and may lead to uncontrolled brain hypoxia. Such states are frequently encountered by individuals experiencing hysteria during hysterical episodes. They can also arise during vigorous running, jumping, cycling, or intensive swimming. This condition results from rapid physical fatigue and a lack of physical stamina. The prevention of uncontrolled hyperventilation involves regular engagement in various forms of physical and physiological exercise. Among the initial signs of hypoxia are anxiety and the loss or absence of bodily sensations. The prevention of these states is possible by suspending and holding one's breath until sufficient accumulation of carbon dioxide in the blood and brain tissues occurs.

Hyperventilation as a Breathing Technique

Hyperventilation, as a breathing technique, is one of the oldest methods for inducing altered states of consciousness. The holotropic breathing technique is performed in a lying position, occasionally changing one's posture depending on personal comfort. The preferred position is lying on one's back, but participants often transition to a lateral or even prone position. Most breathing sessions occur in this manner. Over an extended period, we observed individuals who practiced hyperventilation techniques with reasonable regularity, engaging in 5–10 hour-long sessions per month. We did not detect any adverse physiological changes in their bodies. The immediate effects of breathing techniques varied among participants but largely included increased relaxation, bodily lightness, and euphoric states. Occasionally, participants reported experiencing muscle spasms and cramps, especially in the limbs. These symptoms were often short-lived and transient, typically dissipating within minutes after the completion of the breathing process.

Regular practice of hyperventilation techniques increases the overall tone of the body, enhances endurance, and increases work capacity. It has been observed multiple times that there is a reduced need for extended periods of rest and sleep. A sustained positive psychological and emotional outlook is maintained for longer periods. It is important to note that during the initial sessions of holotropic breathing, rebirthing, and initial diving experiences for beginners, hyperventilation symptoms are often observed. This occurs due to the body's adaptation to a new breathing regimen. As individuals gain experience in breath control techniques, hyperventilation symptoms tend to disappear.

During many sessions of holotropic breathing and rebirthing, deep psychoemotional material from the unconscious mind is frequently brought to the surface. In many cases, the personal experiences that surface may trigger negative reactions. Consequently, the hypothalamic-pituitary system activates, releasing a significant amount of pituitary hormones into the bloodstream. The adrenal glands also release a substantial amount of adrenaline, which in turn converts to norepinephrine. This leads to involuntary vasoconstriction and muscle contraction. Physically, an individual may feel constrained and tense throughout their body, eventually resulting in a sense of disorientation and fatigue.

With the correct execution of the breathing technique, in the first 5–10 minutes, carbon dioxide losses amount to approximately 30-50 fluid ounces (1–1.5 liters) out of the total 4000 fluid ounces (30 gallons) (120 liters) present in the entire body. Breathing intensity, which exceeds the normal breathing rate by 2–3 times, ensures the smoothest, lightest, most tranquil, and comfortable transition into an altered state of consciousness. Starting from the 10-minute mark of intensive breathing (hyperventilation), compensatory physiological mechanisms of the body are activated, gradually slowing down the carbon dioxide loss processes.

Thus, carbon dioxide losses within 10 minutes of hyperventilation are regulated by the physiological homeostasis of the body at the biochemical process level. Hyperventilation induces spasms in the blood vessels of the brain, which prevent excessive removal of carbon dioxide from brain tissues because blood flow to the brain tissues decreases during hyperventilation.

This limited blood supply inhibits the cerebral cortex and activates deeper brain structures that contain old childhood memories, various emotional imprints from the perinatal period in the womb, and genetic memories accumulated over generations. Symptoms such as weakness, tetany, and mild euphoria may occur. This process reproduces an altered state of consciousness, which we can observe through patient feedback and EEG brain scans.

The transition to anaerobic metabolism, with the formation of metabolic byproducts such as pyruvate and lactic acid, is a significant process. Lactic acid is an excellent substrate in oxidative processes, primarily in the cardiac muscle, for energy production. Surprisingly, even under intense physical exertion and heightened psychomotional experiences, angina attacks are practically nonexistent.

When compensatory physiological mechanisms of homeostasis come into play, hyperventilation and associated breathing can only maintain the achieved level of carbon dioxide concentration in the blood and its content in the cerebral cortex. At this point, carbon dioxide losses cease. In total, approximately 80 to 100 fluid ounces (2.5 to 3 liters) of carbon dioxide are lost, which is not critical for the human body. Upon returning to the natural breathing cycle, all indicators return to their initial values.

The depth and penetration into altered states of consciousness primarily depend on the intensity and intervals of breathing during the first 10–15 minutes of the process of entering an altered state of consciousness.

The activation of compensatory physiological mechanisms of homeostasis leads to a healing effect. With regular hyperventilation practice, the nourishment of the cardiac muscle improves, kidney stones dissolve, and cerebral blood circulation improves due to the formation of additional collateral blood vessels. These vessels develop as a result of regular brain training through sessions of hypoxia.

Afterword

The descriptions of altered states of consciousness obtained by the participants in the Holotropic breathwork group may inspire readers to contemplate the boundless and intricate nature of the experiences that reside within each of us. Therapy techniques are sometimes capable of elevating not only the information about our childhood traumas in our consciousness but also, at times, authentic transpersonal poetry that unveils the uncharted depths of our creative and multifaceted unconscious. Everyone is free to choose their own attitude toward such experiences. During the process of psychotherapy, the very act of uncovering, its actualization at the conscious level, is highly significant and meaningful. This sets in motion the psychodynamics of an individual's personality, during which a person gains the opportunity to free themselves from various pains and negative emotions accumulated throughout their life. They can also connect with the experiences that exist within us but, for various reasons, cannot manifest in the context of regular social activities. Psychotherapy can reveal new horizons of personal growth, and what exactly to do with what has been uncovered in the therapeutic process is a challenge for each recipient. There are no clear maps for this journey. Each person may encounter an experience that has yet to be charted on their worldview map. In the Middle Ages, uncharted territory on maps was labeled "Hic sunt dracones" (lat.)—"Dragons live here," signifying the space destined for exploration. In our view, the primary purpose of therapy is to aid in the exploration of the dragons residing within each of us, and we hope that this book can provide some knowledge capable of assisting on this journey.

Bibliography

1. Grof, S. (2008). The Ultimate Journey: Consciousness and the Mystery of Death. Moscow: AST. (Philosophy).
2. Grof, S. (2003). Spiritual Emergency: When Personal Transformation Becomes a Crisis. Moscow: AST. (Texts of Transpersonal Psychology).
3. Grof, S. (2000). Beyond the Brain: Birth, Death, and Transcendence in Psychotherapy. 3rd ed. Moscow: Institute of Transpersonal Psychology, Institute of Psychotherapy Publishing.
4. Grof, S. (2001). Call of the Jaguar. Moscow: AST.
5. Grof, S. (2007). When the Impossible Happens: Adventures in Non-Ordinary Realities. Moscow: AST.
6. Grof, S. (2015). The Cosmic Game: Exploration of the Frontiers of Human Consciousness. Moscow: Ganga.
7. Grof, S. LSD Psychotherapy.
8. Grof, S. (2004). Transpersonal Vision: Healing Possibilities of Unusual States of Consciousness. Moscow: AST. (Philosophy).
9. Grof, S. (2003). The Stormy Search for the Self: A Guide to Personal Growth Through Transformational Crisis. Moscow: AST. (Texts of Transpersonal Psychology).
10. Grof, S. (1994). Realms of the Human Unconscious: Observations from LSD Research. Moscow: MTM.

11. Grof, S. (2001). Psychology of the Future: Lessons from Modern Consciousness Research. Moscow: AST. (Texts of Transpersonal Psychology).
12. Grof, S. (2008). Journey of Self-Discovery. Moscow: AST. (Philosophy).
13. Grof, S. (2004). Consciousness Revolution: A Transatlantic Dialogue. Moscow: AST. (Philosophy).
14. Grof, S. (2018). Holotropic Consciousness: Three Levels of Human Consciousness and Their Influence on Our Lives. Moscow: Ganga. (Transpersonal Psychology).
15. Grof, S. (2002). The Human Encounter with Death. Moscow: AST.

A Brief Message from the Author

Mastering complex psychotherapeutic theories and practices can be a challenging journey. By sharing your experience with this book, you can guide others who are on the same path. Your review could inspire someone to take the next step in deepening their knowledge and applying these insights to make meaningful changes in their life.

Thank you for your support and for taking the time to share your thoughts! Your feedback helps us refine our offerings and empowers others in their pursuit of mastering psychotherapy. If this book has been valuable to you, I'd be grateful if you could take a moment to leave a review. **Your positive rating would mean a lot!**

To share your feedback, simply scan the QR code or click the link below: psychemaster.com/recommends/review-breathwork-therapy-seminar

About the Author

Dr. **Artem Kudelia**, a psychologist with a PhD and a practicing therapist, has extensive expertise in integrative approaches. He possesses comprehensive knowledge of a wide range of psychotherapeutic methods, including humanistic and existential theories, as well as the practical application of cognitive-behavioral therapy (CBT) to effectively address issues such as anxiety, depression, obsessive thoughts, compulsions, social phobias, and complex emotions. His books are valuable resources for professionals and individuals interested in managing their mental health. In addition to managing symptoms, he helps his clients toward self-actualization in various aspects of their lives, including social, career, and personal aspects.

You can connect with me on:

- https://facebook.com/psyche.masters
- https://instagram.com/psyche.masters
- https://threads.net/@psyche.masters
- https://youtube.com/@psyche.masters
- https://tiktok.com/@psyche.masters
- https://pinterest.com/psychemasters

Subscribe to my newsletter:

https://psychemaster.com/early-reader-signup

Also by Artem Kudelia PhD

The ***Psychology & Psychotherapy Theories & Practices*** series offers a detailed examination of the history, theoretical foundations, and practical applications of fundamental approaches in psychotherapy. It is an indispensable resource for psychologists, medical professionals, psychology students, and anyone interested in understanding these complex subjects.

Additionally, the ***Cognitive Behavioral Therapy Self-Help Guide: 15 Steps to Mental Health*** series provides actionable guidance for overcoming various psychological challenges, such as anxiety, depression, excessive anger, obsessive thoughts, compulsions, social phobias, health anxiety, and intricate emotional struggles. These topics were chosen because many individuals facing these challenges often lack awareness of the underlying dynamics. By gaining insight into these processes, individuals can make informed decisions about seeking help, reinforcing the idea that knowledge is a powerful tool for personal empowerment.

Together, these series offer invaluable resources for those interested in psychology, whether for academic study or personal development, by providing comprehensive insights and practical tools that contribute to improved mental well-being.

Psychotherapy Fundamentals Complete Guide

Are you struggling to understand complex psychotherapeutic theories?

Psychotherapy Fundamentals: Complete Guide simplifies the intricate world of psychotherapy, making it accessible and actionable for those interested in self-discovery, self-education, and readers with a wide range of interests.

♥ **Imagine confidently navigating psychotherapeutic real-world scenarios with ease.**

This book is your *comprehensive roadmap to achieving a deep and practical understanding of psychotherapy*. You'll learn to simplify complex theories and integrate them effectively into your life and practice.

Gain a comprehensive understanding of various therapeutic approaches, including *provocative* therapy, *humanistic* therapy, *somatic* therapy, *existential* therapy, *drama* therapy, *psychedelic* and *post-psychedelic* therapy, *anti-psychiatric* therapy, and *integrative* therapy. Each chapter delves into the key themes and methods of these psychotherapy modalities, broadening the horizons for those interested in self-discovery, self-education, and lifelong learning.

▼

https://books2read.com/Psychotherapy-Fundamentals

Hypnotherapy Fundamentals
Complete Guide

Are you ready to uncover the secrets of hypnotherapy?

This comprehensive guide immerses you in the ***theory** and history of hypnosis*, providing a solid foundation for understanding the principles underlying hypnotherapy.

Explore the various techniques and approaches used in *hypnotherapy* ***training*** through ***practice exercises***, including the art of *suggestion* and deepening *hypnotic trance states*, the creation of therapeutic propositions, and the utilization of the power of the subconscious mind.

Learn how to effectively apply *hypnotherapy techniques* to address a wide range of issues, from managing stress and anxiety to overcoming phobias and habits.

Gain an understanding of the transformative potential of hypnosis and its applications for personal growth and well-being.

Unlock the secrets of harnessing the power of the mind and creating positive changes in yourself and others.

https://books2read.com/Hypnotherapy-Fundamentals

Psychology of Love & Death
Therapeutic Path to Fundamental Balance in Life and Relationships

How to Achieve Fundamental Balance in Life and Relationships?

Explore dualistic nature of human consciousness, along with the profound impact of seeking balance between fundamental continuums of *love and death*, *instinct and spirituality, masculinity and femininity* in shaping our experiences and relationships.

Explore the psychopathological profiles and manifestations of love and death, including profiles such as hysteria, paranoia, psychopathy, and others.

Uncover different types of love, from eros to agape, and study the *three-component Theory of Love.*

Familiarize yourself with *real-life psychotherapy cases* that illustrate the complexities of love, death, and therapy and gain *valuable insights* into the human experience and its challenges.

https://books2read.com/Psychology-of-Love-and-Death

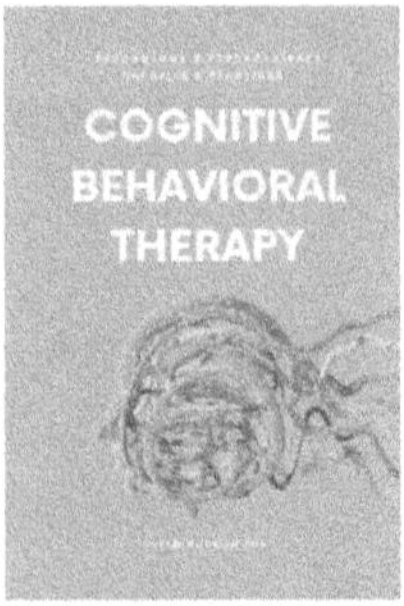

Cognitive Behavioral Therapy
Managing Anxiety and Depression

Explore the roots of anxiety and learn why it's a fundamental aspect of the human experience.

An in-depth exploration of *Panic Disorder*, addressing the irrational fears associated with it.

Examine the nuances of *Social Anxiety* and its impact on personal and professional spheres.

Dive into the world of *Obsessive-Compulsive Disorder*, unraveling its complexities.

Understand the genetic predispositions and learn effective strategies to manage obsessions and compulsions.

Explore *PTSD* from its roots to its biological manifestations. Delve into the trauma cycles, and discover therapeutic techniques for stabilization and overcoming trauma.

Grasp the degrees of *Depression*, from mild to severe, debunking common myths.

▼

https://books2read.com/Cognitive-Behavioral-Therapy

Psychotherapy
Introduction to Healing Vectors

Do you want to understand the variety of methods of psychotherapy and choose the one that is best for you?

In the vast world of psycho-technologies, there are numerous methods of psychotherapy that encompass a wide range of *personality theories* and concepts.

Drawing upon an integral framework, the book maps out the complex *landscape of psychotherapy*, encompassing vectors such as *psychoanalytic*, *hypnotic*, *provocative*, *humanistic*, *behavioral*, *existential*, *transpersonal*, *cognitive*, *somatic*, *psychodramatic* and *psychedelic* therapies, among many others.

This book will provide you with valuable knowledge that will allow you to choose the most suitable therapeutic path for specific circumstances and personality types.

▼

https://books2read.com/Psychotherapy-Introduction

Provocative Therapy
The Healing Power of Dark Humor

Who said that psychotherapy can't be hilariously funny?

Explore innovative ideas about the power of humor in psychotherapy and coaching.

Uncover the archetypal foundation of Provocative Therapy inspired by the myths of the Trickster and the Holy Fool.

Delve into the transformational potential of *Group Provocative Psychotherapy* and the important rules that define successful group dynamics.

Explore the effectiveness of *Provocative Coaching* and its focus points.

Dive into the fascinating world of *Provocative Drama* and its role in therapeutic interventions.

Explore the *pathopsychological profiles*, including *hysteroid, paranoid, psychopathic, obsessive-compulsive, schizoid, epileptoid, schizophrenic,* and *manic-depressive* profiles.

▼

https://books2read.com/Provocative-Therapy

Humanistic Therapy
From Crisis to Self-Actualization

Do you want to explore a world where people are seen as unique holistic systems with infinite potential waiting to be discovered?

Immerse yourself in the theories and practices of humanistic therapy and explore the *transformative path from crisis to self-actualization.*

Unlike psychoanalysis, which focuses on internal complexes and personal traumas, humanistic therapy emphasizes the *study and development of positive personality qualities.*

Humanistic philosophy has also influenced fields such as *education*, promoting *empathy* and *support* as the foundation of learning.

This holistic approach recognizes the *interconnectedness of mind, body, and spirit* and seeks to stimulate personal *growth* and *well-being*.

Take the first step towards self-awareness, personal growth, and a more fulfilling existence.

▼

https://books2read.com/Humanistic-Therapy

Somatic Therapy
The Wisdom of the Body

Would you like to establish a connection with your body and access the source of wisdom?

Unleash the transformative power of *somatic therapy* and embark on a journey of *self-discovery* and *healing.*

Explore the profound connection between the *mind and body.*

Discover the *seven levels of muscular armor* and their connection to specific emotions such as sadness, anger, and fear.

By exploring different body segments, you will unlock *powerful techniques* for releasing pent-up emotions and promoting harmony throughout the organism. From *eye movements* and *jaw exercises* to *deep breathing* and *body movements*, this book offers *practical methods* for *accessing the wisdom of the body* and *restoring emotional balance.*

Acquire unique knowledge about *healing after birth trauma and psychosomatic medicine.*

▼

https://books2read.com/Somatic-Therapy

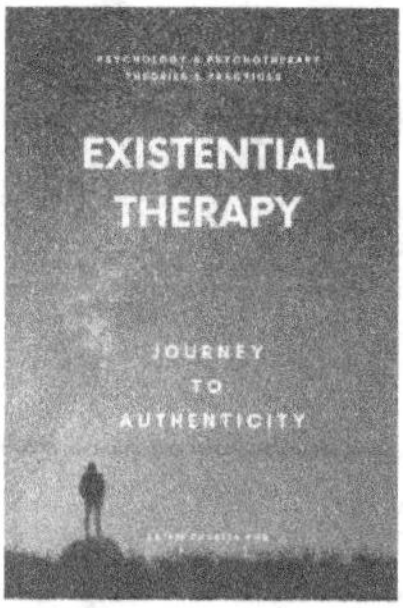

Existential Therapy
Journey to Authenticity

Do you want to know who you really are? What is your personal meaning of existence?

Embark on a *transformative journey* to uncover your *true essence* and embrace the *principles* of existential therapy.

Explore the rich philosophical roots of *existential psychotherapy* and find your path to *personal authenticity.*

Explore key themes such as *freedom, responsibility, meaning,* and *choice*, and learn to courageously and authentically navigate the complexities of existence.

This book provides *practical ideas and techniques* for *applying the principles of existential therapy* to your own life.

Gain a deep *understanding* of your *values, beliefs*, and *desires*, and learn to *embrace uncertainty* and *transform* life's *challenges* into *opportunities* for *growth* and *self-discovery.*

▼

https://books2read.com/Existential-Therapy

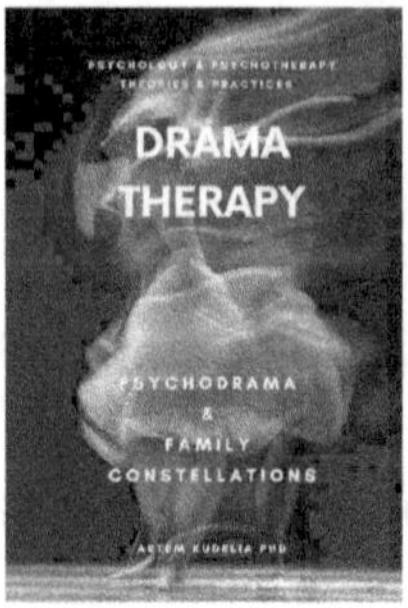

Drama Therapy
Potential of Psychodrama and Family Constellations

Explore the unique world of drama therapeutic approach!

Therapeutic model of intervention that encompasses 12 *powerful speech patterns* capable of significantly *influencing conscious and unconscious processes.*

Through *psychodramatic techniques* and *family constellations*, you will *gain practical knowledge* to enhance your therapeutic practice.

Addressing a wide spectrum of *psychopathological profiles*, including *hysteria, paranoia*, and *obsessive-compulsive disorders*, this book equips you with effective dramatherapeutic activities and psychodynamic exercises.

It serves as a *comprehensive guide* to *crisis intervention, counseling theory*, and *strategies for addiction rehabilitation.*

Gain an understanding of the right hemisphere and the *neuroscience* underlying drama therapy, and learn to *navigate complex emotional situations* with *understanding* and *acceptance.*

https://books2read.com/Drama-Therapy-Constellations

Psychedelic Therapy
The Healing Power Therapeutic Journeys

Embark on a transformative journey into the world of psychedelic therapy!

Explore the fascinating *history* of *psychedelic substances* and potential benefits of working with consciousness-altering substances in clinical practice.

Learn comprehensive information on various *psychedelic therapies*, including *ketamine therapy*, *psilocybin*-assisted psychotherapy, *MDMA*-assisted psychotherapy, and *ibogaine* psychotherapy.

Gain knowledge about *mental health* in the *perinatal period*, the *role of hypnosis*, and the transformative power of *holotropic breathwork.*

Understand the profound impact of *psychedelic medicine* and the potential of *psilocybin microdosing.*

Explore the therapeutic applications of *ketamine* in the *treatment of depression* and *psychosynthesis in coaching.*

https://books2read.com/Psychedelic-Therapy-Journey

Beyond Psychiatry
Exploring Anti-Psychiatry Method

Challenge traditional psychiatry and psychotherapy!

This book presents an *alternative to conventional* ideas of normalcy and offers a *fresh perspective on psychological disorders*, inviting readers to question existing paradigms.

Delve deeper into *psychopathological profiles* and *anti-psychiatric* forms of psychotherapy, examining various profiles including *hysteria, paranoia, psychopathy*, and more.

Gain an understanding of the intersection of psychotherapy and existential philosophy, *challenging the myth of mental illness* within families.

Explore the *treatment of psychosis, trauma*, and *emotional disorders from a holistic perspective.*

▽

https://books2read.com/Beyond-Psychiatry

Integrative Therapy
Personal Transformation Guide

Discover the Power of Integrative Therapy and Embark on a Journey of Personal Transformation!

This book challenges traditional divisions in *therapeutic approaches* and explores the potential of *combining multiple vectors* to create a *comprehensive and integrated therapeutic system.*

Immerse yourself in the world of *neuro-linguistic programming* (NLP), *cognitive styles, neurological levels*, and *integral philosophy*, among other concepts.

Explore practical methodologies such as *shifting negative thinking*, *creating rapport*, and using linguistic patterns to facilitate positive change.

Unlock the transformative *power of anchors*, *changing personal history* and *submodalities.*

Gain an understanding of maps of the world and the *metamodel* for *effective communication.*

https://books2read.com/Integrative-Therapy

Theory & History of Hypnosis
Exploring Altered State of Mind in Trance

Immerse yourself in the fascinating world of hypnosis and explore the history and theory of altered states of consciousness!

This book sheds light on *historical trance practices* and the *role of shamanism*, tracing its influence on *modern psychospiritual orientations.*

Discover the benefits of this book by exploring the *history of trance practices and hypnotherapy.*

Explore the *evolution* of *shamanism*, its connection to *religion*, and its pre-religious *philosophy*, which offered deep insights into the structure of the universe and the mysteries of the spiritual world.

Discover various *hypnotic phenomena* and *states of consciousness* that can be induced in a trance state.

Explore their potential applications in *psychotherapeutic practice*, from *pain management* to the *treatment of depression.*

Learn techniques such as *self-hypnosis, deep trance induction*, and *guided healing visualizations.*

▼

https://books2read.com/Theory-and-History-of-Hypnosis

Hypnotherapy Training
A Guide for Practicing Hypnotherapists

Uncover the secrets of hypnotherapy and improve your practical hypnosis skills!

This book explores *techniques* and *practical skills* for hypnotherapists.

Dive into the depths of the *subconscious* and discover the *transformative potential* of hypnotherapy.

Discover the benefits of this book, which delves into key topics and approaches in *hypnotherapy training.*

Explore developed techniques, including rapport-building practices and the use of matching postures, movements, and breathing with the client.

Engage in exercises that enable the attainment of different trance levels and explore the motives of trance and their application in psychotherapy.

Gain an understanding of different styles and orientations of hypnotic work, from hypnoanalytic and suggestive to behavioral and transpersonal.

https://books2read.com/Hypnotherapy-Training

Healing Anxiety and Overthinking
Proven CBT Strategies for Lasting Relief

Are you exhausted from the relentless cycle of anxiety and overthinking?

Discover the 15-step program that will transform your mental health and bring peace of mind.

Millions of adults struggle with anxiety and overthinking, feeling trapped in a cycle of worry and stress. But it doesn't have to be this way. "*Healing Anxiety and Overthinking: Proven CBT Strategies for Lasting Relief*" offers a comprehensive guide to breaking free from the grip of anxiety using practical, proven **Cognitive Behavioral Therapy** (**CBT**) strategies.

♥ ***Imagine waking up every day with a clear mind, free from the constant barrage of anxious thoughts***

This book is your roadmap to achieving that transformation in just 15 steps. You'll learn to understand the nature of your anxiety, identify its triggers, and apply effective techniques to manage and overcome it.

Take Control of Your Mental Health

Don't let anxiety and overthinking rule your life. With "*Healing Anxiety and Overthinking*," you'll gain the tools and confidence to achieve peace of mind and live the life you deserve.

Mastering Intrusive Thoughts
Practical CBT Techniques for Managing OCD

*Is **OCD** ruling your life with intrusive thoughts and compulsions?*

Take back control with scientifically-proven CBT techniques designed to help you regain peace of mind.

Millions of adults struggle with obsessive-compulsive disorder (OCD), caught in a relentless cycle of intrusive thoughts and compulsive behaviors. "Mastering Intrusive Thoughts" is your step-by-step guide to breaking free from the grip of OCD using practical, evidence-based Cognitive Behavioral Therapy (CBT) techniques.

♥ ***Picture yourself waking up with a calm, focused mind, no longer burdened by the constant anxiety of unwanted thoughts.***

In this book, Dr. Artem Kudelia offers a clear and actionable path to mastering your thoughts in 15 manageable steps. Whether you're new to CBT or have tried other methods without success, this guide provides the tools you need to finally achieve relief.

✔ **Take the First Step Towards Mental Freedom**

You'll gain the knowledge and confidence to conquer your **OCD** and reclaim your peace of mind.

The Anger Solution
A CBT Program for Emotional Balance

Are you tired of living with persistent anger and overwhelming stress?

Discover a practical, 15-step program designed to bring lasting peace and transform your emotional health.

Millions of adults struggle with anger and stress, feeling trapped in a cycle of frustration and tension. But it doesn't have to be this way. "The Anger Solution" offers a comprehensive guide to breaking free from the grip of anger using practical, proven Cognitive Behavioral Therapy (CBT) strategies.

♥ ***Imagine waking up every day with a calm mind, free from the constant barrage of anger and stress.***

This book is your roadmap to achieving that transformation. With clear, actionable steps, you'll learn to understand the nature of your anger, identify its triggers, and apply effective techniques to manage and overcome it.

✔ **Take Control of Your Emotional Health**

With "The Anger Solution," you'll gain the tools and confidence to achieve emotional balance and live the life you deserve.

Health Anxiety Mastery
30 Proven CBT Steps to Peace of Mind

Is health anxiety controlling your life with constant worry and fear?

Regain peace of mind with proven CBT techniques designed to help you overcome health-related anxiety and reclaim control.

Millions of people struggle with health anxiety, trapped in a cycle of physical symptoms, endless reassurance-seeking, and intrusive thoughts about their well-being. "*Health Anxiety Mastery*" offers a clear, step-by-step approach to breaking free from these patterns using practical, evidence-based Cognitive Behavioral Therapy (CBT) techniques.

♥ **Imagine waking up each day calm and confident, no longer overwhelmed by fear and obsessive thoughts about your health.**

In this book, you'll find 30 actionable steps to help you reduce anxiety, challenge limiting beliefs, and develop healthier thought patterns. Whether you're just beginning your journey or have tried other approaches without success, these practical tools will guide you toward lasting relief.

✔ **Start Your Journey to Balanced Mental Health**

How to Get Over Social Anxiety
CBT Strategies for True Confidence and Deep Connection

What if 15 proven steps could free you from social anxiety and help you connect?

Uncover a 15-step CBT program to overcome fear, stop avoidance, and build true self-confidence. Millions struggle with social anxiety, but you don't have to face it alone. This guide provides a clear, evidence-based path to transforming your social life and connecting authentically.

♥ **Imagine engaging in conversations fearlessly and forming genuine relationships free from judgment or rejection.**

With insights from proven cognitive-behavioral techniques and relatable examples, this book offers the practical tools and encouragement needed to face your fears and succeed socially.

✔ **Begin Your Journey to Confidence**

Start transforming fear into connection and reclaim control of your social life with "*How to Get Over Social Anxiety*."

Discover More by Artem Kudelia

Scan the QR code or click the link to access his author page and full collection. Each book provides detailed insights and practical guidance, exemplifying his contributions to psychology and psychotherapy.

books2read.com/Artem-Kudelia-PhD

www.ingramcontent.com/pod-product-compliance
Lightning Source LLC
LaVergne TN
LVHW022227200926
848481LV00006B/2163
9798230585855